OHIO COU...
WHEELING, W. ...3

P9-EMP-070

LIBERIA

Patricia Levy & Michael Spilling

OHIO COUNTY
WHEELING, W. VA. 26003

J
966.62
Levy
2009

Marshall Cavendish
Benchmark
New York

1270228485

MAR 1 3 2009

PICTURE CREDITS

Cover photo: © Jacques Jangoux / Alamy

alt.TYPE / REUTERS: 28, 70, 71, 89, 112, 123 • Bes Stock: 3, 5, 6, 46, 56, 97 • Bjorn Klingwall: 17, 31, 42, 102, 110, 115, 116 • Bruce Coleman Limited: 16, 41 • Charles D. Miller III: 10, 12, 35, 36, 60, 63, 75, 78, 82, 83, 94, 100, 103, 104, 105, 109, 117, 120, 121, 128 • Corbis: 24, 29, 48, 49, 53, 106 • David Keith Jones: 11 • Francis Tan: 131 • Getty Images: 1, 23, 30, 32, 33, 51, 55, 64, 65, 80, 81, 88, 90, 111, 113, 114, 124, 125 • Hutchison Library: 45, 57, 72, 79, 84, 91 • iAfrika: 25, 76 • Karen Lange: 74, 126 • Liba Taylor: 4, 59, 66, 107 • Lonely Planet Images: 38, 40, 58, 67, 86 • National Geographic: 15, 47, 52 • Norfiszuwaan Mohd Ahbar: 130 • North Wind Picture Archives: 19, 20, 21 • Panos Pictures: 7 • Photolibrary: 13, 34, 39, 54, 69, 96, 122, 129 • Stuart R. Gagnon: 44, 85, 87, 101 • Susanna Burton: 18, 68, 108, 127 • Sylvia Cordaly: 14 • TopFoto: 8, 26, 37, 61, 73

PRECEDING PAGE

A group of smiling village children.

Publisher (U.S.): Michelle Bisson
Editors: Deborah Grahame, Mindy Pang
Copyreader: Tara Koellhoffer
Designer: Geoslyn Lim
Cover picture researcher: Connie Gardner
Picture researcher: Thomas Khoo

Marshall Cavendish Benchmark
99 White Plains Road
Tarrytown, NY 10591
Website: www.marshallcavendish.us

© Times Media Private Limited 1998
© Marshall Cavendish International (Asia) Private Limited 2010
® "Cultures of the World" is a registered trademark of Times Publishing Limited.

Originated and designed by Times Media Private Limited
An imprint of Marshall Cavendish International (Asia) Private Limited
A member of Times Publishing Limited

Marshall Cavendish is a trademark of Times Publishing Limited.

All rights reserved. No part of this book may be reproduced or utilized in any form or by any means electronic or mechanical, including photocopying, recording, or by an information storage retrieval system, without permission from the copyright owner.

All Internet sites were correct and accurate at the time of printing. All monetary figures in this publication are in U.S. dollars.

Library of Congress Cataloging-in-Publication Data

Levy, Patricia, 1951-
    Liberia : by Patricia Levy & Michael Spilling. — 2nd ed.
        p. cm. — (Cultures of the world)
    Summary: "Provides comprehensive information on the geography, history,
      wildlife, governmental structure, economy, cultural diversity, peoples,
      religion, and culture of Liberia" — Provided by publisher.
    Includes bibliographical references and index.
    ISBN 978-0-7614-3414-6
    1. Liberia — Juvenile literature. I. Spilling, Michael. II. Title.
DT624.L48 2009
966.62—dc22   2008028788

Printed in China
7 6 5 4 3 2 1

CONTENTS

A girl getting her hair plaited by her mother.

Liberians are an open-hearted and warm people, despite the hardships they have undergone in recent years.

INTRODUCTION

LIBERIA, AN INDEPENDENT REPUBLIC on the west coast of Africa, gets its name from the Latin word *liber*, which means "free." Its foundation in 1822 as a home for freed black slaves from the United States bears testimony to its name and its motto: "The love of liberty brought us here." Today, after almost two decades of civil war and political instability, Liberia is a country seeking to rebuild its infrastructure and economy and to create a country where people can thrive in peace and prosperity. However, peace remains fragile, and the high crime rate, widespread poverty, and poor public services remain a challenge to the newly elected government of Ellen Johnson-Sirleaf (who became president on January 16, 2006).

Despite the problems of recent years, Liberia is a beautiful country that is rich in natural resources, where rare species of animals live in some of the most unspoiled areas of rain forest in West Africa. The challenge for modern Liberia is to harness these abundant natural resources without ruining the environment in the process. Liberians have undergone terrible ordeals in recent years, but they are now emerging from the troubled times with a new commitment to peace and progress. This book in the *Cultures of the World* series celebrates this new beginning.

GEOGRAPHY

LIBERIA IS LOCATED ON THE west coast of Africa, a few degrees north of the equator. It is bordered by Sierra Leone in the northwest, Guinea in the north, the Ivory Coast in the east, and the Atlantic Ocean in the south and west.

Most parts of the country are made up of Precambrian rocks, the Earth's oldest rocks. The Precambrian era began with the formation of Earth some 4.6 billion years ago and ended around 570 million years ago. Liberia's metamorphic rocks (gneiss and schist) and igneous rock (granite) form the West African Shield, a rock formation that is about 2.7 to 3.4 billion years old.

Above: **Liberia's rain forest is the largest expanse of its kind in West Africa.**

Opposite: **Liberia is home to many beautiful beaches, including this one just outside Monrovia, the country's capital city.**

The land in Liberia falls into three main regions: coastal lowlands, plateaus, and highlands. Most of the land located inland from the coastal strip is covered by tropical rain forest. Although it is threatened by deforestation, Liberia's rain forest remains the largest in West Africa (it constitutes 40 percent of West African rain forest).

The first national census, taken in 1984, recorded a population of 1 million. The last census, taken in 1990, showed a population of 2.5 million. Even though the present population estimate is 3.8 million, this does not indicate a very high population density, given the size of the country.

In the past, the relatively small population slowed economic growth. In the late 1950s, for example, when diamond mines were producing a rich yield, the government closed down some of the mines because the increased need for miners was drawing laborers from coffee plantations and iron ore mines. However, this is no longer an issue as Liberia seeks to rebuild its economy after a devastating civil war. The main center of population is found around the capital city of Monrovia.

RIVERS

Some of Liberia's rivers help form the country's national boundaries. The Mano, also called Bewa or Gbeyar, rises in the Guinea Highlands, northeast of Voinjama, and forms more than 90 miles (145 km) of the Liberia–Sierra Leone border. In the east, the Cavalla—also called Cavally, Youbou, or Diougou—originates north of the Nimba Mountains in Guinea and flows south, forming more than half of the Liberia and Ivory Coast border. The Saint Paul River marks Liberia's border with Guinea for part of its journey. One important river that traverses the entire width of the country, the Lofa, has its origin in Guinea.

Like the Lofa, several other rivers flow more or less parallel with one another from the north toward the sea. The 125-mile (200-km) Saint Paul is the most important river, reaching the Atlantic fairly close to the port at Monrovia. The river is an important source of water for agricultural land in the interior, but it is not a convenient source of transportation to and from the capital's port. This is because the Saint Paul, like most of the country's rivers, has several rapids and waterfalls inland, where the gradient of the river is steep, with rocky stretches closer to the coast, making navigation difficult in places. In addition, seasonal rainfall, followed by rapid runoff from the rivers, causes sudden changes in water levels. The Saint Paul is navigable for 18 miles (29 km) upstream from the coast, while the Cavalla can be navigated for 50 miles (80 km) from its mouth in the Gulf of Guinea.

The force of the river has been used to generate hydroelectric energy on the Saint Paul and on the Farmington River, a tributary of the Lofa.

COASTAL LOWLANDS

Liberia's coastline, which is 10 to 25 miles (16–40 km) wide, has many estuaries (the wide part of the rivers located near the sea) that are formed by rivers rising in the north. Wave action has caused long sandbars to form in front of the shallow lagoons (bodies of water cut off from a larger body by a reef of sand or coral) and mangrove (trees and shrubs that grow in saline coastal habitats in the tropics and subtropics) marshes off the coast. The sandbars keep shifting, and this, along with the rocky nature of many of the rivers draining into the sea, means that there are no natural harbors. Since the coastline is fertile, settlements have grown up along it. The largest cities—Monrovia, Marshall, and Buchanan—are on the coast.

HILLS AND PLATEAUS

Plateaus are areas of high and level ground, and in Liberia, they gradually rise from a series of rolling hills with foothills close to the coast. The hills were the first places to be mined for iron ore and were once far more important to the country's economy than they are today. The plateaus have an average height of just under 1,000 feet (305 m), though those farthest inland rise above 1,500 feet (457 m).

Opposite: **The Saint John is one of several rivers running parallel to one another, flowing from the north toward the Atlantic Ocean.**

The Nimba Mountains are located where the borders of Liberia, the Ivory Coast, and Guinea meet.

Some parts of the plateaus remain relatively unexplored because of dense, impenetrable rain forests and rivers that are not easily navigated. Parts of the hilly country, on the other hand, are home to many of the country's biggest coffee plantations.

The highlands rise to about 4,000 feet (1,219 m) above sea level and continue across all three of Liberia's borders. In the northeast they cross over into Guinea, where they form the foothills of the Guinea Highlands. Farther east they include the Nimba Mountains and cross over into the Ivory Coast and Guinea. Mount Nimba at Guest House Hill (5,748 feet/1,752 m)—the highest peak in Liberia—is close to the point where

Total area:	43,000 square miles (111,370 sq km)—slightly larger than the state of Tennessee
Coast measure:	360 miles (579 km)
Land boundaries:	985 miles (1,585 km)—shared with Guinea for 350 miles (563 km), the Ivory Coast for 445 miles (716 km), and Sierra Leone for 190 miles (306 km)

A coffee tree with beans and flowers. Some of the country's largest coffee plantations are found in the hills.

the borders of the Ivory Coast, Guinea, and Liberia meet. At the western end of these highlands are the Wologizi Mountains, close to Sierra Leone. Not surprisingly the mountainous regions of the highlands are the least developed and least populated parts of the country.

CLIMATE

Because Liberia lies just north of the equator, daily temperatures range from 79 to 90°F (26–32°C). Combined with a relative humidity that averages 88 percent, the temperature makes most days extremely hot and sticky. Although there is a rainy season, rainfall is irregular. The rainy season begins earlier on the coast than it does in the interior. The wet season, when relative humidity reaches as high as 95 percent, is between May and November. Usually around July or August there is a brief period that resembles the dry season of December to April.

One of the few respites from the high humidity of this equatorial climate comes toward the end of the year, when the dust-laden desert winds known as the *harmattan* blow from the Sahara region toward

A fertile stretch of land in Liberia. Moderate temperatures and high humidity ensure lush vegetation in the country all year-round.

western Liberia. This dry season has been lengthened by almost a month in recent years, due to deforestation and drought in the Sahel—a vast semidesert region north of Liberia.

There is heavy rainfall along the coast, since it is there that the rainy season begins earliest. Cape Mount records as much as 205 inches (521 cm) of rainfall every year. The northwest coastal region receives a fairly high amount of rain, recording 160 inches (406 cm) annually, while the southeast coastal region receives an average of about 100 inches (254 cm). In the interior the average annual rainfall is about half that of the coastal regions.

The relative humidity is also lower away from the coast. During the dry season days are still hot, but not unpleasantly so, and nights are comfortably cool. Across the country, rain usually falls in long and heavy downpours that may last from a few hours to two or three days.

MONROVIA

The capital city of Liberia, Monrovia, is situated on the coast and is spread across an area divided into a number of small islands by lagoons. Monrovia was founded in 1822 on the left bank of the Saint Paul River on the ridge formed by Cape Mesurado. Because it is situated at a height, it offers a panoramic view of the Atlantic Ocean and the coastal plains.

Monrovia and its suburbs occupy 5 square miles (13 sq km). The layout of the city, which follows a neat grid pattern, reflects the North American origins of the first settlers who designed Monrovia. Some of the older buildings are reminiscent of the old architecture of the southern United States.

The main port and center of industrial activity is on Bushrod Island, which benefits from a deepwater harbor that was constructed between 1944 and 1948 with U.S. aid. Apart from a main wharf (a platform built out from the shore into the water and supported by piles to provide access to ships and boats) where large ships can load and unload, there are specially built piers for shipping iron ore. In addition, there is an oil jetty (a protective structure made of stone or concrete that helps prevent a beach from eroding). Roberts International Airport is 35 miles from Monrovia.

The population of Monrovia is cosmopolitan and includes all of the country's ethnic groups, as well as refugees, other Africans, Lebanese, and other Asians and Europeans.

Liberia's capital was originally named Christopolis, but it was renamed Monrovia in honor of U.S. President James Monroe (1758–1831), whose famous Monroe Doctrine announced that the United States would oppose further European imperial ambitions in the Americas.

The leopard is mainly nocturnal, but it sometimes basks in the sun.

The rarest animal found in Liberia is the Liberian mongoose (Liberiictis kuhni), which was thought to be extinct until a live male was captured in 1989. Even if a female is found to mate with the male, the species will remain highly endangered.

WILDLIFE

Liberia has 193 species of mammals that include various members of the cat family. The leopard, one of the smaller big cats, is the largest cat found in the country. It can grow up to 6 feet, 6 inches (198 cm) in length, including the tail. Its prey includes monkeys. The number of leopards in Liberia, as elsewhere, is decreasing, but there is no shortage of monkeys in the country. Monkeys share the rain forest with animals such as the chimpanzee, antelope, elephant, and anteater. Also found in the rain forest are scorpions, lizards, at least eight varieties of poisonous snakes, and many unusual birds and bats. Three types of crocodile live along the banks of Liberia's rivers.

Two of Liberia's rarer mammals are the manatee and the pygmy hippopotamus, the latter being mainly confined to Liberia, with small numbers found in the neighboring countries of Sierra Leone, Guinea, and the Ivory Coast. Manatees are aquatic herbivorous mammals, which have been overhunted for their meat. The West African species of manatee,

There are many chimpan-zees found in the forests of Liberia.

Trichechus senegalensis, is far less common than it once was. Hippopotami are some of the largest land mammals, but the pygmy hippopotamus, *Hexaprotodon liberiensis*, is a modest 5- to 6-foot-tall (1.5- to 1.8-m-tall) mammal that is found only in the wilds of West Africa. The larger species of hippopotamus spends far more time in the water and is more likely to travel in herds than is its Liberian relation, but both types feed on grasses and reeds, and travel many miles along the river at night.

The rain forest environment and the coastal habitat support a richly diverse bird life. Parrots, hornbills, and woodpeckers are common in the forests, and along the coast flamingoes search for small animals and algae in the muddy waters of the lagoons. The flamingo uses its crooked bill to filter its food from the brackish water.

The political instability that has plagued Liberia in recent years has resulted in poor control over poaching, and this has contributed to the growing number of animal species now facing extinction. Elephants, bush cows, and leopards are slowly but steadily disappearing from Liberia.

PLANT LIFE

The rubber tree is one of the most important trees in Liberia because of its economic value. The average rubber tree grows to about 81 feet (25 m) and yields a milky white fluid called latex, from which rubber is produced. Early in the 20th century a British-German company began to produce rubber for export from wild rubber trees in Liberia. It was not long before a plantation was created and thousands of rubber trees were planted. The first plantation was eventually forced to close down because of falling world rubber prices, but when the market improved in the mid-1920s, the Firestone Tire and Rubber Company acquired the plantation and expanded it to about 1 million acres (405,000 ha).

Another economically important tree is the coffee tree, and more than one species flourishes in Liberia. Until Brazil began to dominate the market

The thunbergia is just one of the several species of flowers that fill Liberia's forests with a splash of color.

in the late 19th century, Liberia's economy was bolstered by the export of coffee from the indigenous species *Coffea liberica*. This species is still cultivated in the coastal region, but it produces an inferior type of coffee that has a bitter taste. In the north of the country, the imported species *Coffea robusta*, which is largely used in the manufacture of instant coffee, is far more common.

The kola tree, native to tropical Africa, is also found in Liberia. It is popular for its nuts, which provide a source of caffeine when chewed. There is a small export trade of kola nuts to Guinea.

Latex is collected by cutting into the bark of the rubber tree and collecting the flow in a small cup. Each cut yields only a tablespoonful of latex, but a new cut can be made every other day. The trees are then periodically left to renew themselves.

RUBBER PRODUCTION

Latex is collected from a rubber tree in a small cup. When a sufficient amount of latex has been collected, it is mixed with water and acid is added to help the particles of rubber adhere to one another. This allows the rubber to be compressed by a machine, and the sheets of rubber that emerge from the machine's rollers are then dried.

HISTORY

VERY LITTLE IS KNOWN about the people who inhabited the land that became Liberia in the early 19th century. The country is Africa's oldest independent republic. It dates back to 1822, when U.S. philanthropic organizations succeeded in establishing an African home for former slaves. These groups were partly inspired by Britain's efforts to settle former slaves in Sierra Leone, but an attempt to do the same with former U.S. slaves slowed down after the death of Paul Cuffee, who started the project.

In 1816 the United States began to negotiate with local rulers to acquire enough land to form a settlement for freed slaves. The following year the American Colonization Society was founded with the intention of resettling emancipated slaves and free-born Africans. By 1821 the society was able to purchase the area around Cape Mesurado, later renaming the settlement Monrovia. Within a year the first settlers arrived from the United States, and in 1824 the name *Liberia* was adopted.

The name Liberia *stands for "liberty" or "land of the free."*

Left: **An artist's sketch of Monrovia in the 1880s.**

Opposite: **The liberation monument in Monrovia.**

EARLY HISTORY

When the Sahara region began to dry up, around 2000 B.C., some of the area's inhabitants are believed to have moved south and penetrated into West Africa. Liberia's first inhabitants were probably the descendants of these people. It is also thought that Mande-speaking tribes migrated to Liberia from regions that now belong to Ghana and Mali. Kru tribes are thought to have been among the earliest of these arrivals, coming sometime after A.D. 1000.

After A.D. 1400, waves of immigration saw new tribal groups moving into Liberia—the Krahn, Grebo, Gio (also known as Dan), and Mandingo from the Ivory Coast; the Mano from Ghana; and the Vai from Sierra Leone. The Bassa, Dei, Kpelle, and Kissi also arrived around this time. The reasons for these population shifts are not fully known, but the conquest and decline

The slaves who were transported to the plantations of the European colonies in the Americas had to endure severe hardships along the way. They were crowded into the lower decks of slave ships and they barely had room to move.

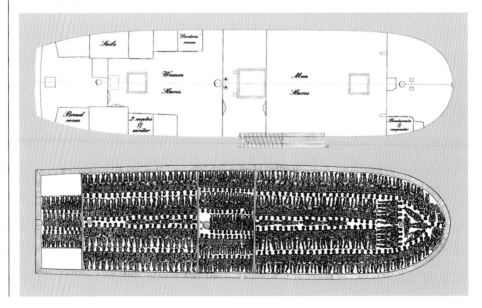

of the ancient empire of Ghana (in modern Mali and Mauritania) may have led some groups to flee south to escape Muslim conquerors. These groups brought with them the skills of iron smelting, cloth weaving, and cotton spinning, as well as important new crops such as rice.

The identity of the first Europeans to reach Liberia has not been established. Hanno, a Carthaginian navigator who lived in the fifth century B.C., made an exploratory voyage down the west coast of Africa, but French traders in the 14th and early 15th centuries are thought to have been the first to trade with the Africans living there. In 1461 a Portuguese mariner named Pedro de Sintra reached the coast of Liberia and paved the way for later Portuguese explorers, who largely restricted themselves to mapping the coastline, since the inland rain forest presented a formidable natural barrier. Early traders were interested in the Liberian coast because that was where they collected melegueta peppers. Years later the British and French came to the Liberian coast to collect slaves.

Liberia has benefited from the support of the United States ever since the country declared itself a republic in 1847.

GRAINS OF PARADISE

The Africans in what is now Liberia first made contact with Portuguese traders because of the Portuguese people's need to add flavor to the dull food they stored dry for consumption during the winter months. *Aframomum melegueta* (melegueta pepper), a plant that belongs to the ginger family and is native to parts of West Africa, bore seeds that were used as a spice and a medicine. They were so highly valued that they were known as grains of paradise, and in time, part of the coastal area of Liberia became known as the Grain Coast. Christopher Columbus sailed to Sierra Leone for the Portuguese and very likely traded for pepper along the Grain Coast.

PAUL CUFFEE

Paul Cuffee (1759–1817), a rich Quaker (a member of the Religious Society of Friends) of African-American and Native-American descent, made his fortune in shipping. He was one of the first people to support the concept of financing former slaves who wanted to leave the United States and settle in Africa. His idea was to make one trip every year with settlers and cover the costs by bringing back African produce for sale in the United States. In 1816 he carried through his plan and landed in Freetown, Sierra Leone, with nearly 40 former slaves on his ship, *Elizabeth*. He died the following year, however, and although his plans seemed to have died with him, he had succeeded in convincing people of the viability of his project. Groups such as the American Colonization Society took up his dream and made it a reality.

FOUNDING A COUNTRY

In 1808 the United States declared the slave trade illegal, and in the early 19th century, the Grain Coast was suggested as a possible home for freed slaves. In 1818, less than 10 years after abolition of the slave trade, two U.S. government officials journeyed across the Atlantic with representatives from the American Colonization Society, and together they held discussions with African tribal chiefs. These talks were unsuccessful at first, but in 1821 an agreement was signed between the society and the local African ruler Peter, allowing the society to buy some land. The following year the society and six other like-minded philanthropic organizations supervised the first repatriation of freed black slaves to Africa. At this point the territory was a relatively small area in the vicinity of what is now Monrovia.

A white American who played an influential part in Liberia's early history as a nation was named Jehudi Ashmun (1794–1828). At the age of 24 he wrote a report for the American Colonization Society that called for renewed efforts to continue the work of Paul Cuffee. He arrived in Liberia in 1822 and remained there until his death in 1828. He set about adding new territory to the colony, and within three years he had negotiated a new treaty with local tribal chiefs. He also helped establish a system of government and encouraged the development of a rudimentary form of commerce. At the same time other settlements were being founded along the coast by other philanthropic organizations; the

A young Liberian girl touches the monument that depicts Liberia's beginning as a colony for African Americans.

towns of Greenville and Harper were established in this way. Various state-based colonization societies in Mississippi, Virginia, and Maryland also helped launch colonies for freed slaves. One of these, the Republic of Maryland, was first settled in 1834 under the guidance of the Maryland State Colonization Society. In 1838 other African-American settlements were united into the Commonwealth of Liberia. In 1839 the first governor, Thomas Buchanan, was appointed. When he died two years later he was replaced by an African named Joseph Jenkins Roberts, who had been born free in Virginia. Under Roberts the territory expanded, and in 1847 Liberia announced its independence from the American Colonization Society and officially declared itself an independent republic. In 1857 a separate colony that had also been founded by one of the philanthropic groups, called "Maryland in Liberia," with its capital at Harper, joined the new state of Liberia.

The 1821 sale of land by the African king Peter was made after American Robert Stockton held a pistol to the king's head.

There remained some disagreement with the colonial powers of Britain and France over the location of the new country's borders, because these two countries had vested interests in the states that neighbored Liberia. By 1919, however, the last of these differences, with France, were resolved. The exact boundaries agreed upon in 1919 are the ones that continue to define Liberian territory to this day.

An artist's impression of President Joseph Jenkins Roberts's home in the 1870s.

Liberia was one of the first African countries to sign up to be a member of the League of Nations in 1920—the precursor to today's United Nations.

MONEY PROBLEMS

Until its declaration of independence in 1847, Liberia received cash subsidies from the colonization societies that had been involved in the country's establishment. This source of funding could not continue indefinitely, and when the aid stopped, the country faced financial ruin. For the next 80 years Liberia turned to European nations for assistance. Britain provided a huge amount of money as a loan in 1871, and a British-German company established the first rubber plantation in 1926.

A lack of investment and money compounded the problems that faced the first settlers. Without adequate provision for training them in new skills, the former slaves were left to their own resources. For many of them, the challenge of adopting a rural African lifestyle and abandoning the American culture in which they had been brought up proved to be very difficult. The fact that the indigenous African inhabitants did not readily accept the new arrivals made matters worse. Many of the new settlers gave up trying to make a living from agriculture and turned instead to trade in coffee, sugar, palm oil, and cocoa.

These difficulties caused the national debt to increase every year. The relatively healthy trade in the export of coffee to northern Europe suffered a setback in the years after Liberian coffee was introduced into Brazil, the South American country that eventually came to dominate the world market in coffee exportation. The 1870s witnessed a worldwide fall in the prices of cocoa and sugar, and this brought on an economic crisis that plagued Liberia for nearly 60 years.

A signboard at the Firestone rubber plantation, which is the largest of its kind in the world.

NATIONAL RECOVERY

In 1926 the U.S. tire-making giant Firestone established a rubber plantation near Monrovia. It was the largest rubber plantation in the world, and it remained the country's biggest employer for the next 45 years. Liberia received an annual grant from the company, and a huge loan secured through the company went toward settling Liberia's outstanding national debts.

In the 1920s the American-owned Firestone Plantation Company helped modernize the Liberian economy.

25

The United States helped in the construction of a deepwater harbor on Bushrod Island.

In the 1920s Liberian bosses were accused of sending Africans as virtual slaves to plantations in Spanish Guinea. The president (Charles Dunbar Burgess King) resigned over the issue, and a new administration was formed under President Edwin James Barclay (1882–1955) in 1930. Further financial difficulties led the League of Nations—a forerunner to the United Nations (UN)—to offer a new assistance package, which was eventually accepted in new discussions with Firestone.

WORLD WAR II

Liberia was affected significantly by World War II, though not in the way most countries were. In 1942, Liberia and the United States signed a defense agreement that changed Liberia's previously insignificant role on the world political stage to a prominent one. The agreement was made because the Japanese invasion and occupation of Southeast Asia denied the West its main source of rubber. Apart from Ceylon (modern-day Sri Lanka), the only remaining source of natural rubber available to the United States and its allies was the Firestone plantation in Liberia, and rubber was urgently needed for the war effort.

The terms of the defense agreement resulted in the United States investing in the development of Liberia's transportation infrastructure. Roads were built, and an international airport and deepwater harbor were constructed in Monrovia. Liberia was not involved in the war militarily, and it was not until January 1944, after the election of William Vacanarat

Shadrach Tubman as president, that the country officially declared war on Japan and Germany.

Confirmation of the growing involvement of the United States in Liberian affairs came when the U.S. dollar replaced the former British-backed currency as Liberia's legal tender. Liberia's signing of the UN declaration in 1944—it was one of only four African nations to sign up to be a member of the new United Nations—symbolized its emergence as a fully fledged independent nation, although one that had close ties to the United States.

PEACE BEFORE THE STORM

In 1960 Liberia served a two-year term as a nonpermament member of the UN Security Council. When the Organization of African Unity (OAU) was formed three years later, Liberia was one of the founding member states.

From 1943 to 1971 William Tubman was Liberia's president. When he died in office his vice president, William Richard Tolbert Jr. (1913–80), assumed the presidency. The new president faced economic problems arising from a fall in world prices for rubber and iron ore, but on the world stage Liberia was heralded as a stable African nation that was uniquely able to effect a peaceful and constitutional transfer of power. Most other areas of Africa were experiencing turbulent times.

When the government increased the price of rice in 1980, a number of antigovernment demonstrations took place, and leaders of an opposition party were imprisoned when they called for a general strike. Within a month Tolbert was killed in an army coup and Liberia's hope for stability was rudely shattered. The new leader was Samuel Kanyon Doe (1951–90), who was a master sergeant in the army when he assumed power at

Half a million Liberians became refugees in neighboring countries as the country drew closer to civil war in 1990.

Government forces fire at rebel forces trying to enter Monrovia in Liberia.

Ellen Johnson-Sirleaf became the first democratically elected female head of state in the history of the African continent when she was elected president of Liberia in 2006.

the head of a new People's Redemption Council. Part of the reason for the violent overthrow of Tolbert's government was that the Americo-Liberians, people who descended from the former slaves who came to Liberia in the 19th century, held most of the political power. The majority of Liberians belonged to the various indigenous tribes that had long lived in this part of West Africa, and they had become increasingly disappointed with governments that were dominated by Americo-Liberians.

CIVIL WAR

The People's Redemption Council claimed to be uniting the country, but the constitution was suspended and political parties were banned. Elections were held in 1985, but it is generally agreed that the results were rigged to ensure the election of Doe as president. He formally took over in 1986.

In 1989 a rebel army based in Sierra Leone and led by Charles McArthur Ghankay Taylor (b. 1948) crossed into Liberia. A bitter struggle between various ethnic factions followed. Doe was largely supported by the Krahn and Mandingo, while Taylor's army was mostly made up of the Gio and Mano. Some order was restored when the Economic Community of West African States (ECOWAS) organized a peacekeeping force. Taylor retaliated by establishing his own capital in Gbarnga and proclaiming himself president. Doe was killed by a group belonging to another rebel leader, Prince Johnson.

PEACE AT LAST?

The civil war dragged on, with no one side able to achieve a decisive military advantage or come to a lasting agreement with its political opponents. In 1993 the UN negotiated a treaty between the main factions, but the provisional government failed to carry out the terms of the treaty. In 1995 there was another attempt at a truce, and the armed factions agreed to a peace deal.

The civil war seemed to have ended at last with the signing of the Abuja Accord (a peace treaty) in 1996. About 30,000 to 60,000 fighters gave up their weapons. On July 19, 1997, in a vote judged fair by international observers, Charles Taylor was elected president of Liberia. However, Taylor's regime was brutal and oppressive, targeting opposition leaders and human rights activists. Taylor proved to be an unpopular leader, and in response to his government's incompetence, a new civil war started in 1999. The war intensified in 2003, with fighting raging on the streets of Monrovia. Taylor was forced to flee to Nigeria as the country descended into chaos. A transitional government took power later that year. In 2006 Taylor was extradited from Nigeria to Sierra Leone, where he faced a war crimes tribunal. He was later tried for a variety of war crimes in the international war crimes court in The Hague, Netherlands. His trial is still ongoing.

In 2005 Liberia held its first democratic elections in many years, and Ellen Johnson-Sirleaf was declared president in January 2006. Since Johnson-Sirleaf's election, peace has returned to the country and reconstruction of the country's economy and infrastructure has begun after decades of civil strife.

Refugees fleeing the country at the onset of the civil war in Liberia.

In 2007 there were almost 15,000 UN peacekeepers stationed in Liberia. They have done much to improve security and curtail lawlessness in Liberia.

GOVERNMENT

THE GOVERNMENT OF LIBERIA has only recently reasserted its power after years of mismanagement under the leadership of Charles Taylor and a 14-year civil war that left the country in ruins. After two years of being run by a transitional government, today Liberia has a new democratically elected government with a new president, Ellen Johnson-Sirleaf, at the helm.

Liberia's earliest constitution followed the example of the United States but denied the majority of the population many of the constitutional rights that should have been extended to them. The indigenous tribes were not treated as equals, and a political elite developed among the early Americo-Liberians and their descendants. Under the presidency of Tubman (1943–71), some attempts were made to deal with this problem by extending the vote to all adults, including women, who paid taxes and owned property. This was not universal suffrage, and although it was a step forward, it made little difference to most Liberians.

President Tolbert's government (1971–80) underwent a more progressive change. Universal suffrage was introduced, and the constitution was amended so that no president could stand for re-election. It turned out to be too little, too late, and the military takeover launched by Doe was supported by those who thought a new and fairer system of government would emerge. A new constitution was drawn up in 1984, but it was not very different from the preceding one, and controversy over Doe's election as president robbed it of much of its legitimacy.

Above: **The William Tubman Monument in Monrovia. Tubman, a lawyer by profession, worked as a county attorney, judge, and preacher before becoming president.**

Opposite: **A woman casting her vote during the 2005 presidential elections in Liberia.**

A sign encouraging the people to vote during the 2005 elections.

Ellen Johnson-Sirleaf worked for both the UN and the World Bank before becoming president of Liberia.

THE ELECTIONS OF 2005

The civil wars of the 1990s and the early years of the 21st century undermined Liberia's government and democracy. However, since the end of the Taylor regime, the country has become more peaceful and stable. President Johnson-Sirleaf was elected for a six-year term in 2006, with 60 percent of the vote. The runner-up in the presidential election was former European Footballer of the Year 1995 George Weah, who won 40 percent of the vote. Weah claimed that he had lost because of election fraud, but this allegation has never been proven and observers judged the vote to be fair.

The president is both the head of state and the head of the government, as well as commander in chief of the armed forces. Presidents may not serve for more than two six-year terms.

THE SENATE AND THE HOUSE OF REPRESENTATIVES

Liberia has a two-chamber system of government. The National Assembly consists of the 30-seat Senate and a 64-seat House of Representatives. Members of both chambers are elected by popular vote. Members of the

Senate serve a nine-year term, while members of the House of Representatives serve six-year terms. Power in both chambers is currently shared by seven main parties and a number of independent representatives. These parties include the Alliance for Peace and Democracy (APD); the Coalition for the Transformation of Liberia (COTOL); the Congress for Democratic Change (CDC), which is led by George Weah; the Liberian Action Party (LAP); the Liberty Party (LP); and the National Patriotic Party (NPP). Elections for both chambers are due to be held next in 2011.

THE TRUE WHIGS

From 1878 until the coup in 1980, political power was in the hands of the True Whig Party. No other political party in the world has managed to remain in power uninterrupted for so long. The party was named after a British political party called the Whigs, which dominated the politics of Britain in the 18th century.

The True Whig Party was the preserve of the Americo-Liberians, and it was through this party that the Americo-Liberians retained control of the National Assembly. It was the only organized political party in Liberia for many years, but it maintained the appearance of needing popular support by a series of nomination conventions for the National Assembly, at which "candidates" were "elected"—although most of the decisions were actually made by the ruling elite long before the conventions took place. There were no limits on the sums of money that local businessmen could give to the party, and civil servants had "contributions to the party" deducted from their salaries. The National Assembly had a Senate and a House of Representatives, but over time the two chambers became little more than debating clubs because the True Whigs always had a majority and the president was always a member of the party.

Main opposition candidate and national hero George Weah.

33

20TH-CENTURY HEADS OF GOVERNMENT

Year	President
1900 to 1904:	Garretson Wilmot Gibson
1904 to 1912:	Arthur Barclay
1912 to 1920:	Daniel Edward Howard
1920 to 1930:	Charles Dunbar Burgess King
1930 to 1943:	Edwin Barclay
1943 to 1971:	William V. S. Tubman
1971 to 1980:	William R. Tolbert, chairperson of People's Redemption Council
1980 to 1986:	Samuel K. Doe President
1986 to 1990:	Samuel K. Doe
1990 to 1996:	A state of civil war with different regions of the country controlled by various armed factional groups
1997 to 2003:	Charles Taylor, chair of Council State
1995 to 1996:	Wilton G. S. Sankawulo
1996 to 1997:	Ruth Perry, chair of transitional government
2003 to 2005:	Charles Gyade Bryant
2006 to present:	Ellen Johnson-Sirleaf

Right: **Ellen Johnson-Sirleaf** began her term as president in 2006.

Opposite: **A Dan chief.** Tribal chiefs are important links between the central government and the villages.

LOCAL GOVERNMENT

Local government for most of the country is based around 15 counties: Bomi, Bong, Gbarpolu, Grand Bassa, Grand Cape Mount, Grand Gedeh, Grand Kru, Lofah, Margibi, Maryland, Montserrado, Nimba, River Cess, River Gee, and Sinoe. Every county has one administrative official who is appointed by the central government, and there is no elected local council. Monrovia is governed directly by the national government, and there are also two territories that, like the counties, are broken down into various districts. The districts are subdivided into a number of smaller administrative regions, each of which is under the rule of a tribal chief.

The tribal chiefs are important links between the central and the local governments. One of the chiefs' responsibilities is the functioning of the tribal courts, where local disputes are aired and misdemeanors are handled.

HUMAN PAWNS

In parts of Liberia, the local government continues to be dominated by the members of small but powerful families. Behind the power lies wealth, and in this sense, little has changed over the centuries, but in the past wealth was acquired and maintained by a process of owning people that was close to a state of domestic slavery. It was known as pawning and occurred when someone exchanged either him- or herself or one of his or her children for a sum of money or valuable possessions, such as farm animals. In return, the person who was pawned was committed to work for the lender until the debt was paid. A clan leader or tribal chief could demonstrate his wealth and influence by building a large pool of pawns.

LOCAL CHIEFS

Tribal chiefs continue to play an important role in the local government in Liberia. Until the troubles in the 1980s and the civil war in the 1990s, most Liberians living outside of the capital had experienced government only in the form of village meetings under a tribal chief. A recent development has been the establishment of paramount chiefs who govern a far larger area than before.

Historically the choice of an individual as a local chief was often made from a small number of influential families associated with the role of tribal chief. To some extent age is a factor, with the most elderly members of a prestigious family having a strong claim to leadership. A significant exception to this pattern developed among some of the tribes in the northwest part of the country. This region had a relatively unstable past, and opportunities arose for adventurous groups to achieve tribal power rather than simply being born into it. There was a tradition of slave trading that allowed successful individuals to emerge as leaders who could maintain their position through acquired wealth and force of arms.

A Dan chief standing with the staff of authority on his shoulder.

Opposite: **The Temple of Justice in Monrovia. The Western system of law has functioned effectively in the capital and major towns except during the civil war.**

One of the duties of tribal chiefs is to mediate disputes between villagers. Often disputes are caused by the breakup of a marriage, when the two families are eager to divide the couple's goods to their own advantage. The husband's family wants their dowry, or bride price, back, while the wife seeks to keep it as compensation for her years of work. It is the chief's job to keep all sides happy, since they must all live as neighbors after the divorce is over.

SYSTEMS OF JUSTICE

A system of criminal law based on a Western model, with judges, juries, and courts of law, has always existed in Liberia. The Supreme Court is headed by a chief justice, who is helped by four associate justices. The associate justices are all appointed by the president. The Western system of law has functioned effectively only in the area around the capital and in large towns. There has been a history of politicians manipulating the law to their political and personal advantage.

The civil war saw the collapse of the criminal law system as power passed into the hands of rival groups that established their own summary forms of justice. A major challenge the country faces as it tries to rebuild itself is to reassert a system of justice that goes beyond the imprisonment and execution of political rivals.

In rural areas more traditional methods of tribal law have operated through chiefs and village communities of elders. The traditional forms of justice that exist in these areas depend for their success on the respect that is accorded to tribal chiefs and village elders. The legal precepts are not the result of government legislation, and law books are not consulted when considering a case.

One traditional form of justice that is no longer practiced in Liberia is trial by ordeal. In this custom a person accused of a serious crime would have to go through some painful ordeal as a test of integrity and honesty—for example, drinking a poison made from the bark of the sasswood tree. The belief was that a guilty person would find it difficult to maintain the bluff of innocence when faced with the possibility of death by poison.

In 2007 former president Charles Taylor was charged with war crimes at an international court in The Hague, Netherlands. His alleged crimes include murder, terrorism, sexual violence, enslavement, and cruelty.

ECONOMY

THE MAINSTAY OF LIBERIA'S market economy is agriculture, with seven out of 10 Liberians earning their living on the land. More women than men are engaged in agriculture, although men make up 60 percent of the country's labor force. Others are employed mainly in manufacturing and various types of administration and service. There are no state-owned industries.

One consequence of the country's dependence on agriculture is that consumer goods and raw materials have to be imported on a large scale, mainly from the Far East. The cost of this is somewhat balanced by exports from the mining, forestry, and rubber industries. Other important exports include cacao, coffee, and palm kernels. Restrictions on diamond exports have recently been lifted, since the return of peace in the country. Most exports go to Germany, South Africa, Poland, the United States, and Spain. Liberia's chief imports are machinery, metals,

Left: **Women harvesting rice in Liberia. Liberia's economy is largely based on agriculture.**

Opposite: **A worker stacking bricks in a brick factory in Monrovia.**

textiles, electrical goods, and foodstuffs. Major import partners include South Korea, Singapore, Japan, and China. Liberia has accumulated an external debt of over $3.2 billion dollars (U.S.) and it is believed to be rising. Price inflation currently runs at 15 percent, making goods expensive for ordinary Liberians.

THE LEGACY OF WAR

The 14-year-long civil war did more to weaken Liberia's economy than any other factor, and its long-term effects are continuing. The constant fighting damaged the country's infrastructure, including its roads, bridges, and ports, and because the area around the capital was the center of the political struggle, this was where most of the damage occurred. Unfortunately the area around Monrovia is home to much of the country's industry—a petroleum refinery, cement plants, and factories—and these businesses have suffered considerably from the poor roads and inadequate transportation system. The civil war also left more than three-quarters of Liberians unemployed, although people are slowly returning to work now that peace has been restored.

The fighting also eroded people's confidence in the country's economic future and led to a severe lack of investment both at home and from abroad. Businesspeople, like many other citizens, fled the country, taking with them their skills and capital. Nearly all of the foreign nationals, many of whom were engaged in commercial business, also left. The civil unrest severely dented the tourist trade, and although tourism was never a major economic asset, the war prevented its development.

An abandoned office block being used as housing by the poor in Monrovia.

In the long term, the most damaging consequence of the war was its effect on the country's education system. Because of the economy's reliance on agriculture, before the outbreak of the civil war governments had been developing vocational education programs. Young Liberians were being trained to earn a living in commerce and industry, but the collapse of centralized government brought all such educational programs to a halt.

NATURAL RESOURCES

Liberia's most important natural resource is iron ore. Other natural resources include gold, diamonds, lead, graphite, and manganese. Bauxite, copper, tin, zinc, and barite have also been found. In the early 1980s deposits of uranium were identified in the counties of Bong and Lofah.

Liberia has a very small oil industry. It is widely believed that there are reserves of oil off the country's Atlantic coast. Potential oil fields are in the process of being mapped through agreements with foreign oil companies, but it may be some time before the country is able to exploit this resource. Most of Liberia's oil currently has to be imported.

One resource that is being exploited, though not to its full capacity, is water for generating electricity. Almost half of the electric power used in the country now comes from hydroelectricity. The largest hydroelectricity generating station is on the Saint Paul River, not far from Monrovia.

The sea is also a natural resource, providing a source for mackerel and barracuda, and there are a number of Liberian fishing companies. In recent years several inland fishing concerns that use artificial ponds to breed fish have been established.

The Lamco mines, along with other iron mines, make Liberia one of the leading exporters of iron ore in Africa.

Projects have been launched to raise rice production, and international aid programs have helped in this endeavor.

Firestone's biggest plantation is located at Harbel, where the company has 118,000 acres planted with rubber trees.

The tropical rain forest is a variable source of hardwood timber, and the government operates a system of concessions that gives companies—often foreign-owned—the right to exploit a predetermined area of forest in return for a fee. It was not until the 1970s, however, that the first reforestation programs began, and a substantial proportion of the country's natural forests has been depleted. In recent years, in an attempt to kickstart the economy, the Liberian government has signed deals with steel giant Mittal and the Firestone Tire Company to revive the iron ore and rubber industries. Many Liberians are unhappy with these deals because foreign-owned companies will once again be making profits from the exploitation of Liberia's rich natural resources. However, these companies have invested in the local community by building roads, financing schools, and providing jobs.

FARMING

There are some large farms that are operated as commercial businesses. The owners are often foreign companies, but the managers who run these farms on a day-to-day basis are Liberians. Most farms, however, are small

DOMESTIC ECONOMY: THE COCONUT PALM

A vital component of the village economy is the coconut palm. Its branches are used in house building and thatching. String and raffia are made from the stripped leaves, and from these the villagers make baskets, nets, and even clothes. The fruit is used to make cooking oil, which is the base of palm butter soup. It is also made into candles, soap, cosmetics, and palm wine. The inner nuts are dried to make nut meat that can be stored or sold, while the shells are burned to make ash for soap. Kitchen utensils, brooms, and fences are also made from the palm tree.

and belong to a family. Although these individual farms are small, their total value to the country's economy is equal to that of the large farms.

A typical small farmer grows rice, cassava, and vegetables, and owns animals such as goats, chickens, sheep, and ducks. The animals have a cash value and provide an important source of food for the family's own needs. Farmers also earn cash by cultivating coffee, cacao, oil palms, swamp rice, and sugarcane. Many farmers are members of local cooperatives, and they sell their cash crops to their cooperative, which in turn sells them in bulk to merchants.

The cultivation of rice makes an essential contribution to the feeding of the country's population, but because the yield is low, a significant quantity of rice also needs to be imported every year.

As mentioned earlier, in 1926 the U.S. company Firestone acquired the first rubber plantation in Liberia and expanded it on a large scale. It also established other plantations. It had around 10,000 employees at its two plantations in Harbel and Cavalla. In recent years human rights activists have accused Firestone of exploiting workers by requiring them to deliver excessively large quotas of rubber by working long hours. Observers have also criticized Firestone for keeping workers in unclean and overcrowded living quarters and not providing safe working conditions. Although Firestone is still one of the largest employers in the country, other international companies have now established their own smaller plantations. There are also many independent rubber farmers who plant their own rubber trees and sell the latex to foreign firms that handle the refining process.

In recent years South American drug cartels have used Liberia as a transit point for getting illegal drugs, such as cocaine and heroin, into Europe. Liberia's borders are not closely watched, so drugs are brought by ships across the Atlantic Ocean and landed in Liberia. The drugs are then shipped or flown by small airplanes to southern Europe.

Liberia has the largest foreign-owned fleet of merchant ships in the world. Of the 1,948 ships registered in Liberia, 1,904 are foreign-owned.

A pickup truck converted into a "moneybus," or public car, awaits passengers in Gbarnga.

TRANSPORTATION

An estimated three-quarters of the country's roads are not passable year-round. This problem was compounded by the civil war, during which roads were badly damaged and there was no investment in road building or maintenance. The result is that the country presently has only two reliable routes that can be used by trucks transporting heavy goods. Both highways lead to Monrovia, one from Buchanan and the other from Kakata. There is a vital railroad link, with a total of over 304 miles (490 km) of track, that connects the port with the areas where iron ore is mined. The railway was built by the mining companies, which still own and operate the lines for the transportation of iron ore to the port. When the civil war flared up again in 2003, the railway line became inoperable. Today the government is seeking to get the line working again. There are many

IRON ORE

In the 1960s the production of rubber—until then Liberia's most important industry—fell into second place in Liberia's national economy, behind the mining of iron ore. Large deposits of iron ore were discovered only in the 1940s in the mountainous area that forms the northern border with Guinea. Today iron-ore mining is an important activity in four main areas. The most significant is around Mount Nimba, and the other three are the Bomi Hills, the Mano Hills, and the Bong Range. Iron-ore exports are one of the major foreign exchange earners for Liberia. Steel giant Mittal signed a deal to mine iron ore from the Mount Nimba region in 2006, creating an estimated 3,000 jobs.

small airstrips in the interior, while the international airport, built by the United States during World War II, is situated to the east of the capital.

With Monrovia being a free port, it is common to see large oceangoing vessels around the world declare Liberia to be their country of registration. There are more than 1,900 ships from various nations that carry Liberian registration, which means the country can lay claim to one of the largest tanker fleets in the world. Even though Liberia does not actually own these ships, the country earns valuable foreign currency from the annual fees it is able to charge them.

A form of transportation for both goods and passengers that is common in West Africa is the mammy wagon, a locally made wooden structure with high sides attached to the chassis of a truck. Inside it goods or people can be transported.

Monrovia is the only free port in West Africa. This means that foreign goods can be stored and redistributed to other ships without the payment of duty.

ENVIRONMENT

LIKE SO MANY ASPECTS of life in Liberia, the environment has been neglected amid the strife and destruction of two decades of civil war and political upheaval. Liberia's rich natural resources—especially diamonds and timber—were, in part, a source of conflict, as the warring factions sought to control the products that would finance their military operations. Now that peace has returned to Liberia, environmental issues have become more important than ever. Improving sanitation, water supply, and refuse collection are priorities for President Ellen Johnson-Sirleaf's government.

Unfortunately the civil war and postwar reconstruction meant that logging and farming in the country went uncontrolled for two decades and did serious damage to some of Liberia's valuable rain forests. Since the UN lifted restrictions on the trade of Liberian diamonds in 2007, mining companies have worked with little or no concern for the environment. The Environmental Protection Agency (EPA; an agency charged with protecting human health and safeguarding the natural environment) of Liberia was created in 2003. Despite this positive development, Liberia still lacks trained people who can effectively enforce environmental regulations.

The poor state of the environment has also had a damaging impact on public health. The nation's low life expectancy (40.39 years) is in part a consequence of unsanitary living conditions, poor-quality drinking water, and poor air quality in the cities. The lives, health, and material prosperity of Liberians will not improve until good sanitation and safe drinking water are available to all.

Above: **A baby chimpanzee looks out dolefully from its cage. Like the locals, the animals in Liberia have also borne the brunt of war-torn Liberia.**

Opposite: **A lush patch of rain forest surrounds the Saint Paul River in Liberia.**

RAIN FORESTS AND DEFORESTATION

Until a few decades ago, Liberia was almost completely covered by forest. Today just a third of the country is tropical rain forest. Liberian forests make up 44.5 percent of the remaining unspoiled rain forests in West Africa, including the last two large areas of closed canopy tropical rain forest, which make up part of the once-great Upper Guinean ecosystem and the Congolese forest. Sapo National Park is considered one of the least disturbed areas of primary forest in West Africa. With forests deteriorating in much of West Africa, Liberia's rain forest is of incalculable value.

Liberia's forests are home to numerous native species and many species that are virtually extinct elsewhere in the region. The rain forest supports hundreds of species of birds, nine of which are endangered, as well as rare species of fauna and flora that are unique to West Africa. The Jentink's duiker (the rarest in the world), the pygmy hippopotamus, the Liberian mongoose, and several dozens of reptiles—including three types

In 2007 the Liberia Environmental Watch (LEW; a nonprofit, nongovernmental organization devoted to advocating for Liberia's environmental protection) held its first national conference in the United States in an attempt to raise consciousness about Liberian environmental issues. This was the first of many steps that will be needed in order to improve Liberia's environment.

As food in Liberia becomes increasingly scarce, many forests such as this one have been cleared to make way for farmlands.

of crocodiles and at least eight poisonous snakes—live in Liberia's forests. Although there has been no recent scientific survey of the forest, more than 2,000 different types of flowering plants are believed to thrive in Liberia—240 of which account for valuable timber species and hundreds of which have medicinal value.

The forest also provides an important livelihood for many of the people who live there. It provides shelter for their cultural and religious practices, including animist shrines; traditional bush schools; cover for important water sources; and is home to medicinal herbs. It also provides rural dwellers with income from the trade in arts and crafts. Traditionally rural people looked after the forest by limiting fishing seasons and prohibiting the killing of some animals, such as leopards. The loss of the forest reduces people's ability to feed and look after themselves, and also undermines a way of life that has existed for centuries. As the forest disappears rural communities decline.

Trees in this forest in Liberia are being logged for timber.

FARMING AND LOGGING

One of the most serious challenges facing Liberia is deforestation due to the jungle being cleared to be used as farmland or for logging. In the late 1990s the Liberian government granted massive logging concessions to timber companies that wanted to exploit the forest. This was done to earn foreign currency while trying to reconstruct the country in the aftermath of the civil war. Although the government has since sought to restrict the activities of loggers, logging continues illegally, and the government lacks the means to control it. Tens of thousands of Liberians depend on logging for their livelihoods, so the industry will remain a part of Liberian life

Logging (cutting down trees for timber), along with the export of diamonds, was one of the key sources of money for the warring factions during the 14-year-long civil war.

*The Liberian
government has
set up the Forest
Development
Agency (FDA)
to manage the
development and
protection of
Liberia's
rain forest.*

for the foreseeable future. Most Liberian timber is exported to European markets to be used as building material.

An additional problem is that about 98 percent of the country's energy needs are met by burning fuelwood and charcoal. This means that local wood will remain an important resource for both businesses and homes.

Liberia sorely needs an educational program to teach people how to use the resources of the forests without causing damage. Widespread logging in almost every important forest, including areas previously designated as national parks, has led to 60 percent of the country's forests being damaged or degraded. Sixty species of tree are most affected by the logging, with 10 species—including ekki, niangon, and abura—making up 65 percent of the total. Roads built by logging companies have contributed to the destruction, since they not only damage the forest, but also expose animals to further threats by making access for hunters much easier.

The process of converting forest to farmland began in the 1970s, when large areas of jungle were cleared for the development of coffee, rubber, and oil palm plantations. In the early 1980s Liberia was one of the last West African countries with large areas of primary forest, but recent estimates suggest that some 104,000 acres (42,000 ha) of forest land are transformed into bushland by shifting cultivation farming methods each year. By the mid-1980s the country had also lost over 70 percent of its mangrove swamps. Between 1983 and 1993 Liberia lost 13.2 percent of its forest and woodland areas.

PROTECTED AREAS

Until 2003 only one-quarter of Liberia's forests in Sapo National Park (whose total area is 698 square miles/1,808 sq km) was classified as protected land. This allowed loggers, farmers, and plantations to exploit the majority of the forest without restriction. Recently, however, the government has sought to improve the state of Liberia's forests by designating all of Sapo National Park as a protected area and also creating the Nimba Nature Reserve. The Nimba Nature Reserve is shared by neighboring countries Ivory Coast (Cote D'Ivoire) and Guinea. International conservation organizations have also been invited to Liberia to assess the condition of the nation's biodiversity. At the last count the country was home to 2,200 species of plants, 193 mammals, and 576 bird species.

Before 2003 uncontrolled logging and farming in Sapo National Park did great harm to both the forest and the wildlife of the park. In 2002 conservationists sought to educate people by setting up a forest soccer league from villages around the park to bring about an awareness of environmental concerns. Teams were named after local animals to encourage people to protect and be proud of the environment.

The Grebo Forest Reserve is home to an amazing array of wildlife, including the pygmy hippo and chimpanzee. Conservationists have established a program to protect the chimpanzee, which has been hunted to the point of becoming endangered.

A fisherman cruises along a river in the Tai National Park, which is a UNESCO world heritage site. The forest is one of the last major remnants of the primary tropical forest in West Africa.

FAUNA AND FLORA INTERNATIONAL

Since 1997 Fauna and Flora International has made Liberia the central pillar of its West African program. In 2001 it was the first international

A hunter demonstrates the technique he uses to hunt chimpanzees in the Nimba Mountains of Liberia. While the adults are killed for their meat, the baby chimpanzees are usually sold alive to animal exporters.

environmental group to establish an office in Liberia. The organization played a significant role in supporting the National Transitional Government of Liberia and was responsible for preparing three landmark environmental laws.

The first of these laws expanded Sapo National Park, one of the least disturbed forest ecosystems in West Africa. The second created the Nimba Nature Reserve, the product of an unprecedented transboundary agreement among Guinea, Liberia, and Ivory Coast. The third law reformed Liberia's National Forestry Law, which had initially been drafted to promote logging and was used to devastating effect during the later years of Charles Taylor's presidency. During this time logging and forest disturbance increased dramatically.

ENDANGERED WILDLIFE

The damage to and loss of rain forest has had a serious impact on wildlife in Liberia. The animal population is in rapid decline, and animals such as the pygmy hippopotamus, elephant, and leopard are almost extinct. Sightings of rare animals by villagers are often difficult to confirm, as the surviving population of species seems to be always on the move in search of remaining dense forest regions. In the less densely forested coastal areas, hunting and the conversion of forest to farmland have decimated wildlife, and there are no longer any large herds of big game in the interior of the country. The poaching of wild animals for food has also increased, especially since the roads created by logging operations have made access to the forest much easier than before. Chimpanzees in particular have suffered at the hands of poachers.

THE PYGMY HIPPO

The forests of Liberia are home to the largest populations of pygmy hippopotamus in the world. Less than one-eighth the size of the more common river hippopotamus, the pygmy hippo was first described by scientists in the 1840s based on specimens collected in Liberia. The pygmy hippo is about 5 feet long (1.52 m), 30 to 39 inches (0.76 to 1 m) tall, and weighs between 397 and 605 (180 and 274 kg) pounds. Its black back has a greenish sheen that provides it with camouflage in its habitat of coastal forests, rivers, and marshland. Pygmy hippos can live up to 35 years in the wild.

Pygmy hippos are threatened by a combination of loss of habitat as a result of jungle being cleared for farming and local hunting. Pygmy hippos are solitary and secretive animals, and they spend much more time out of the water than the river hippo. Foraging for food in the forests, they run for the protection of streams or rivers only in times of danger. Their survival is dependent on the existence of protected forests. Conservationists in Liberia consider the pygmy hippo to be the country's most important wildlife species and are working to educate the public

to ensure that the animal survives. However, only the establishment of proper forest reserves will allow the pygmy hippo to thrive.

Many rural Liberians consider the pygmy hippo to be a special animal. They tell stories about a mystical creature that carries a shining stone in its mouth to light its path at night. Another story describes the slippery texture of the hippo's body and how this makes it difficult to capture or hunt. Legend has it that spears, arrows, and even bullets bounce off its magical hide.

In 2004 the International Union for the Conservation of Nature and Natural Resources (IUCN) listed five mammal species as endangered and 10 other species as vulnerable. The endangered animals were the chimpanzee, the Diana monkey, Liberian mongoose, Nimba otter shrew, and the red colobus monkey. Vulnerable animals include the African elephant, Jentink's duiker, the pygmy hippopotamus, spotted-necked otter, and West African manatee.

The Liberian mongoose, a native of Liberia, was first discovered in Liberia in 1958. Little was known about the animal except what was recorded in local legend. The animals were said to live in small groups and to feed on earthworms and various other insects. This rare animal has been seen mainly in the forests of Liberia and the Tai National Park in neighboring

A teenage boy enjoying clean water from a newly made well in Liberia.

Ivory Coast. The civil war has prevented detailed study of the mongoose. However, it is known that the mongoose lives in low-lying areas and has been heavily hunted for food. Sightings are so rare that some conservationists have suggested that the mongoose might be extinct.

WATER RESOURCES AND SANITATION

With its heavy rainfall and small population, Liberia has plenty of water resources. Water supplies usually come from open sources such as streams, swamps, and shallow uncovered wells. Few households have water delivered through pipes, and in rural areas especially, people still walk great distances to fetch water. During the rainy season insects and parasites thrive, creating a major health hazard. Hundreds of thousands of Liberians die each year from water-related diseases.

In urban areas today 79 percent of the population has access to safe drinking water, while in rural areas, just 13 percent has safe water. In 2003, at the end of the civil war, these figures were much lower, so sanitation has improved in recent years. A World Bank report estimates that Liberians use less than 13 gallons (50 l) of water per day, which is less than the minimum amount set by the World Health Organization (WHO) for a basic level of hygiene.

It is generally agreed that the falling life expectancy in Liberia is due to poor health that is caused by poor sanitation and unclean drinking water. Many hundreds of thousands of Liberians still suffer from chronic poverty due to a lack of safe drinking water and proper sanitation, especially the safe disposal of human waste. Most homes do not have indoor plumbing with toilets, and most of the hundreds of public latrines built by the government are broken. Poor sanitation causes cholera and diarrhea, and health-related problems remain one of the great challenges facing modern Liberia.

WASTE AND REFUSE

In the immediate aftermath of the civil war, a 2004 UN report observed that the collection of town and city waste had virtually stopped, leading people to dump their waste in hazardous mountains of refuse or burn it, causing dangerous air pollution. Today Liberia's towns and cities create more than 2 million tons of solid waste each year. Monrovia's 1.6 million inhabitants make more than 700 million tons of solid waste each day, which is much more than the city authorities can handle. There are few proper landfill sites to deal with this refuse; much of it ends up dumped on the streets and roads around Monrovia. Hospitals do not have any proper waste disposal systems, so medical waste—such as syringes, bandages, and human matter—is thrown away in open sites with other town refuse. Some waste is thrown into local rivers, swamps, or along the coast, causing further dangerous pollution to local water supplies.

The Mano and Saint John rivers have become increasingly polluted from the dumping of industrial waste, such as iron-ore tailings, and the coastal waters are becoming heavily polluted from oil residue and the dumping of raw sewage and wastewater.

Ravaged by civil war, Monrovia's collection of waste stopped, causing huge bundles of trash to pile up along the streets.

LIBERIANS

SINCE LIBERIA was created through European-drawn borders from the colonial period, the many ethnic groups that live within its borders are almost accidentally Liberian, and most of the tribal areas cross Liberian borders into other countries. Depending on what criteria one uses to define an ethnic group, there are between 16 and 28 ethnic groups living in Liberia in addition to the Americo-Liberians. Of these just three—the Bassa, Dei, and Bella—are found only in Liberia. All the others exist in greater numbers in other countries.

Mainly because of this ethnic diversity, it is not easy to generalize about Liberians. A city dweller who lives in the capital and is aware of being a descendant of a 19th-century family of freed slaves has a sense of identity that is quite different from that of, say, a Muslim rice farmer from the Kissi tribe living in the interior of the country. What may be said of Liberians as a whole is that they are an open-hearted and warm people.

Typical Liberian teenagers, despite having grown up in a period of civil war with its widespread death and destruction, are far younger at heart than many of their contemporaries in North America or Western Europe. Adult Liberians retain a childlike sense of fun and enjoyment that many of their peers in other parts of the world have left behind in their rush to grow up. Even compared with people in other parts of Africa, Liberians are noted for their infectious enthusiasm for enjoyment.

About 42 percent of Liberia's population lives in urban areas. Liberians can be broadly divided into those who live an urban, Western-style life and those who live the traditional village life in rural areas.

Above: **A group of laughing children. Liberians have a sense of fun and enjoyment despite the years of fighting that they have endured.**

Opposite: **A typical family unit in Liberia.**

An overhead shot of pedestrians in downtown Monrovia.

DEMOGRAPHICS

The population of Liberia, including refugees who have taken up residence in neighboring countries, is about 3.2 million, or about 49 persons per square mile. The population is unevenly distributed, with most people living around Monrovia and in a stretch of land from Monsterrado County to the Guinea border. The chief urban settlements are Monrovia, Buchanan, Edina, Greenville, Harper, Robertsport, and Marshall—all coastal towns. There are about 2,000 villages, mostly in central Liberia, the northwest, and close to Monrovia. In contrast the southeastern forests are uninhabited. Putting aside population shifts caused by the war, the trend of movement is from rural areas to urban, especially to Monrovia. There are also population movements to the enclaves around rubber plantations and iron mines.

The population of Liberia, which increased from about 758,000 in 1950 to 1.5 million in 1974 to the present 3.2 million, is one of the fastest-growing in the world, at almost 5 percent per year. One reason for this

is the negligible emigration of Liberians. Other reasons for the increase are the high birthrate and decreased mortality rate as endemic diseases, although still severe, have been controlled in recent years. Even so the infant mortality rate is high, at 149 deaths per 1,000 live births, and the life expectancy is low—39 years for men and 42 years for women. The low life expectancy is mainly a consequence of the civil wars and the impact they have had on health care and diet, and, of course, the dangers that come with living in a war zone. This produces an unusual age distribution, with many more younger people than elderly: Over 43 percent of the population is under 15 years old, and only 2.7 percent of the population is over age 65. The average family is made up of five persons.

More than 70 percent of Liberians work in farming, while just 8 percent work in industry and 22 percent work in the service sector. While the civil war raged, most Liberians were unemployed, but since peace has returned the economy has again started to create jobs for Liberians. Indigenous Africans make up 95 percent of the population, while Americo-Liberians make up just 2.5 percent, and other groups, such as the Congos (KON-gohs), make up the remaining 2.5 percent.

Refugees fetch water from a well. The war has increased the number of refugees both in Liberia and in the neighboring countries.

The Congos are a group of Liberians who trace their origins to freed slaves from the Congo area who were supposed to be transported to the Americas.

Bassa boys. The Bassa live along the coast and, like the Kru, make good sailors.

THE TRIBES

The government of Liberia recognizes 16 different tribes, although ethnolinguists put the number of tribes at around 28, based on language differences and cultural habits. The indigenous tribes can largely be divided into three ethnolinguistic groups—that is, groups of people who share a common language and customs.

THE KWA-SPEAKING PEOPLE The Kwa-speaking tribes include the Kru, Bassa, Dei, and Grebo. Their traditional homelands are the fertile plains extending along the coast from the Ivory Coast to Monrovia and beyond. The Kru (who make up 8 percent of the population) are well known as good seamen and traders. In the past they dealt in slaves and wore tattoos on their foreheads to identify themselves as Kru and to warn people not to try to enslave them. The Bassa (16.3 percent of the population) live in central Liberia. They live only in Liberia and, like the other members of their language group, they have migrated in large numbers to the urban areas. The Dei (0.5 percent) are a small group. The Grebo (7.6 percent) occupy the extreme southeast of the country.

Two interior tribes—the Krahn (5.2 percent of the population) and the Bella (0.5 percent)—also speak a language related to these groups, although they are traditionally agriculturists and hunter-gatherers rather than seafarers.

THE MANDE-SPEAKING PEOPLE The Mande speakers come from the north of the country and are indistinguishable from tribes of the same name in other West African countries, such as Mali, Guinea, Sierra Leone, and the Ivory Coast. Eight tribes of this group live in Liberia—the Mandingo, Vai, Gbandi, Kpelle, Loma, Mende, Gio, and Mano. Although they are grouped together due to the similarities in their languages, they have very different cultures and traditions. The Mende (0.5 percent of the population) have a strong tradition of masked dancing, while the Loma (5.3 percent) have historically been soldiers in the Frontier Force. The Mandingo (2.9 percent), most of whom are Muslims, are traders. The Kpelle (20.8 percent) are the most traditional of these tribes, having remained hunter-gatherers and farmers. The Vai (2.8 percent) are a coastal group with a literary tradition. They, too, are Muslims and most make their living through subsistence farming, fishing, and craftwork.

THE WEST ATLANTIC SPEAKERS The West Atlantic speakers are a small group of tribes composed of people from the interior who probably came to Liberia from the northwest. They make up about 8 percent of the population. They are mainly rice farmers, and many of them are Muslim.

The Gola and Kissi belong to this group. The Kissi inhabit a belt of hills at the point where Guinea, Liberia, and Sierra Leone meet. They cultivate rice in natural marshland and grow yams, sweet potatoes, and taro. They also grow and sell coffee and kola nuts. Their huts are round and built of clay, and villages are small, with about 150 residents, all of whom are related. At the head of the village is the senior member of the family, who acts as the priest. The Kissi make stone statues of their ancestors. They are also famous for their currency, called "Kissi money"—small twisted iron bars that are no longer in use.

This woman is part of the Gola tribe near Zorzor. The Gola are mainly rice farmers.

61

THE MAJOR TRIBAL GROUPS

Bassa	16.3 percent	Krahn	5.2 percent
Belle	0.5 percent	Kru	8 percent
Dei	0.5 percent	Loma	5.3 percent
Gbandi	2.8 percent	Mandingo	2.9 percent
Gola	4.7 percent	Mende	0.5 percent
Grebo	7.6 percent	Vai	2.8 percent
Kissi	3.4 percent	Other Liberian tribes	0.2 percent
Kpelle	20.8 percent	Non-Liberian tribes	0.9 percent

THE AMERICO-LIBERIANS

Americo-Liberians are the descendants of the 12,000 people who founded Liberia, the freed slaves from the United States who settled there in the 19th century. Most of them migrated between 1820 and 1865. The term *Americo-Liberian* is avoided today, since it implies that this group is still a settler group and not really part of the country. Americo-Liberians make up about 1.5 percent of the population. They are chiefly urban and educated, with a distinct class system of a very wealthy elite that owns estates or businesses, a middle class of clerical people, and a class of poor manual workers. The elite consists of about 1,500 people, making up 3.3 percent of the Americo-Liberian population.

The Americo-Liberian population has grown since the 19th century, either by natural growth or through the integration of indigenous people into the group by means of marriage or adoption. Like their indigenous neighbors Americo-Liberians followed the practice of taking in a local child as a servant, in exchange for support or cash for the parents. Such children were often adopted by the family and absorbed into its culture. Also in the past many Americo-Liberian men followed the local custom of taking second wives. Children by those marriages were legally adopted.

The group also includes about 5,000 people called Congos, who are barely distinguishable from Americo-Liberians. These are the descendants of freed slaves taken from slaving ships captured by the U.S. Navy while sailing from Africa to the Caribbean. *Congo* has become a term of insult for all Americo-Liberians.

Although most Americo-Liberians live in the major towns in the coastal plains, many of them have country houses located well away from the cities. Before the 1990 coup, the Americo-Liberians made up the bulk of the ruling elite in Liberia. They are largely Christian.

OTHER GROUPS

In addition to the Americo-Liberians and the various tribal groups that have always lived in Liberia, there are relatively newer and more temporary settlers who found Liberia's peace and stability an inducement to settle and trade there. Liberia's constitution does not allow non-blacks to become citizens, but people from many countries have become part of the social and cultural life of the country.

Many Ghanaians have settled in Liberia as semi-permanent residents. They are chiefly people from the Fanti tribe, and they are traditionally fishermen who work in the coastal shores. Many of the Fanti have settled in the towns, received an education, and become office workers, adopting the city lifestyle. The Fanti in Liberia are largely literate and make up about 0.5 percent of the population, making their ethnic group as large as some of the smaller indigenous tribes.

Another distinctive group is the Lebanese. Arab traders settled extensively throughout West Africa, and Liberia was no exception. Even in small towns in Liberia, there are stores and restaurants run by Lebanese. Although they are not allowed to become citizens, they have contributed much to the economy of the country.

When the economy was flourishing, foreign companies were encouraged to invest in Liberian industry, and Americans, Spanish,

Although people from many countries have settled in Liberia, the constitution does not allow non-blacks to become citizens.

Dutch, British, Germans, and Swedes worked in Liberia, particularly in Monrovia. They worked as professional advisors, technical experts, teachers, or missionaries. They were evacuated at the beginning of the civil war.

NATIONAL DRESS

When the early settlers came from the United States, they emulated the dress of the wealthy plantation owners of the South, including frock coats, hats, and cravats. These days most Liberians wear Western-style clothing that has been adapted for the humidity and heat.

Traditional dress for women is a wide-necked blouse called a *bubba*, often in colorful designs such as tie-dye, and a full-length sarong, called a *lappas*, in equally vivid colors. At one time portraits of famous African leaders were popular on clothes. Most women wear a headdress made of a scarf tied in elaborate ways. Men wear loose, brightly colored shirts over Western-style cotton trousers.

When they take part in dance festivals, Liberians often cover themselves in white clay and wear long skirts made from grass, dyed and woven tunics, beads, and colorful headdresses.

SOME FAMOUS LIBERIANS

William Vacanarat Shadrach Tubman William Vacanarat Shadrach Tubman, born in 1895 in Harper, was of Americo-Liberian descent. In 1943 he became president, sponsored by the ruling True Whig Party.

A group of Liberian women in their brightly colored headdresses.

Opposite: **William Tubman is regarded as the founder of modern Liberia.**

He was conscious of the divisions in his country, where a tiny elite controlled most of the wealth and power. He began to unite all the tribal groups and encouraged tribal leaders to join the national government. He also carried out a policy of open-door economics, encouraging foreign investment. He died in 1971.

George Weah Another famous Liberian is the soccer player George Weah, who has played for the French soccer team Paris Saint Germain, the Italian giants AC Milan, and the English champions Chelsea. In 1995 he was voted World Player of the Year. After retiring from soccer he attempted to become the president of Liberia, but narrowly lost to Ellen Johnson-Sirleaf in the 2005 election.

ELLEN JOHNSON-SIRLEAF

Ellen Johnson-Sirleaf is Africa's first elected female president. She won the election in 2005 and was declared head of state in 2006. Her nickname, "Iron Lady," comes from her reputation for having an iron will and steely determination. A mother and grandmother, Johnson-Sirleaf has a long political history in Liberia, having been an advisor to Charles Taylor and a political opponent of former president Samuel Doe. She was imprisoned briefly in the 1980s for criticizing Doe. Twice she went into exile to escape political and legal persecution under different Liberian regimes.

Johnson-Sirleaf has a lot of experience in international finance and economics, having worked for the World Bank and the United Nations Development Program in Africa. Many of her admirers believe that this makes her ideal for the massive job of rebuilding Liberia's broken economy and infrastructure. Others believe that Liberia needs a woman to fix the country's problems, since it was warring men who ruined the country in the first place. Her critics, however, believe that she will not be strong enough to deal with the problems that go along with so many former soldiers and fighters becoming civilians.

LIFESTYLE

FOR DECADES LIBERIA WAS the most stable and flourishing country in Africa. Although coups and military governments seemed to be commonplace throughout the African continent, Liberia prospered. When stability ended with Doe's coup in 1980, the causes could be seen in the basic social structure of the country. Liberia was—and still is—divided into two quite distinct ways of life: the tribal life of the villages and the Westernized urban life, which has a social hierarchy with a small elite of wealthy people at the top. Two decades of war and coups have had little effect on that division. But the inequalities that brought about 15 years or so of problems and intertribal warfare still exist. All the factions that have fought over Monrovia have fought for their group to have the biggest share of the gains, not to bring about a fairer system.

Since the end of the war, the process of rebuilding the devastated towns and villages has begun. More than 200,000 refugees have returned to their homes, schools are open again, roads and homes are being rebuilt, and companies are trading. But the process is slow and life is still hard in Liberia. In 2000, 80 percent of the people were living below the poverty line, and this figure has improved only slightly since then.

Above: **A hairdresser runs his salon by the walls of an empty building.**

Opposite: **Liberians who fled their homeland during the civil strife are beginning to return.**

CITY LIFE

Visitors to Monrovia in 1980 might have been forgiven for believing themselves to be in a new state of the United States. The currency was the U.S. dollar, the police officers wore secondhand New York Police Department summer uniforms, and signs outside the larger towns announced their names as New Georgia, Maryland, and Louisiana. On

It is estimated that 250,000 people were killed in Liberia's 14-year-long civil war.

67

The capital has sprawling shantytowns filled with homes made out of cardboard and corrugated iron.

Despite the presence of 15,000 UN peacekeepers, armed bandits still roam the streets of Liberian towns, terrorizing and robbing people.

Saturday nights the nightclubs and bars were lit up, while on Sundays Baptist choirs could be heard. Anyone turning on the radio would hear Voice of America.

Now things are different, largely due to the impact of the war and the changes brought about by the governments. The Liberian dollar has replaced the U.S. dollar, and the nightlife is quieter.

Monrovia is a small capital, with an area of about 5 square miles (13 sq km). It has an interesting mix of architecture, with old Southern U.S.–style mansions and bungalows, now dilapidated, alongside more modern high-rise buildings. Besides these are traditional African huts as well as shantytowns. The population is made up of tribal groups living in small communities. Each ethnic group has developed its own churches and social structures.

Members of the same ethnic group often share the same type of work. The Kru, for example, who live in the coastal towns, work mainly as sailors or as stevedores on the docks, although some have joined the teaching and medical professions, the civil service, and politics. They are organized into clanlike groups, and an organization called the Kru Corporation, founded in 1916, handles disputes between tribespeople and their employers.

The towns have people living in extreme poverty close to others who are very wealthy. The population of the towns is young and there is a high proportion of males to females, as young men migrate from rural areas to the cities in search of work.

Towes have developed along major roads to the big mining and farming estates. Zorzor, for example, is on the main road to Sierra Leone; Kpelle and Loma take their farm produce there. It has a hospital funded and supported by the Lutheran Church of America, a teacher-training college, and some small industries. It is a quiet town, depending on trade and foreign-funded projects, such as the hospital and leper colony. The church is the center of social events. Two-story concrete housing blocks predominate in the modern parts of the town, while typical older homes are rectangular and one-storied, with their walls made of plaited mats or mud and wattle, with tin roofs.

EDUCATION

In the early years of settlement by Americo-Liberians, education for the settlers' children was considered to be of paramount importance. Americo-Liberian children were educated in locally established schools

Pedestrians and vehicles jostle for space on bustling Randall Road in Monrovia.

Street lighting was returned to Monrovia only in 2006, after the government used electric generators to bring light to the capital.

An English class at Saint Mary's High School in Monrovia. Educational standards in Liberia are high by African standards, thanks largely to a well-developed system of schools and the efforts of the U.S. Peace Corps volunteers who teach in many areas.

The University of Liberia is one of West Africa's oldest universities. It was founded in 1862 as Liberia College.

for entrance into professions such as law, theology, and medicine. After elementary school they went to the United States, Europe, or neighboring African countries to complete their education.

There was no provision for indigenous children to go to school, even those living close to the settlements. As time passed schools were set up by various missionary groups. These provided the only education available to indigenous children. By 1939 private or mission schools provided three-quarters of Liberia's elementary education.

Little changed until after World War II, when the government became aware of the need to educate the indigenous children. In 1961 an educational system was set up, which lasted until the civil war began. Nursery school was followed by six years of elementary school, three years of junior high school, and high school. By the late 1960s, 50 percent of schools were financed and run by the government; the rest were privately run facilities and mission schools, in equal numbers. Today slightly less than 50 percent of schools are financed by missionary societies or by the big mining companies for their workers' children. Instruction covers literacy, mathematics, science, and work-oriented programs such as cooking, agriculture, and manual skills.

Despite the disruption of 14 years of civil war, children are slowly returning to school across Liberia, thanks to the presence of the UN peacekeepers. Education is compulsory for children between the ages of six and 16. Elementary and secondary education is free. According to the United Nations Educational, Scientific and Cultural Organization (UNESCO), in 2004, 62 percent of school-age children attended elementary school and only 25 percent attended secondary school, a figure that had dramatically increased since the end of the civil war, when most schools were closed. Rural children have a poor attendance record, since schools in rural areas are widely scattered, there is no reliable daily transportation, and the schools have no dormitory facilities. In addition, the use of English for instruction has made education difficult for rural children. In both rural and city schools the dropout rate is very high: Only one-quarter of the children who start first grade finish sixth grade. Textbooks are expensive, and it has been difficult to get good teachers with the country torn apart by war. Fewer girls attend school than boys, and they often start at a much later age so that by fourth grade many are leaving school to get married. About 25 percent of young people are literate. These figures were much lower during the height of the civil war. Only 53 percent of Liberians over the age of 15 can read and write.

Child soldiers, armed with guns, going on a military drive through the streets of Monrovia.

Further education is largely provided by the University of Liberia in Monrovia, Cuttington University College in Suakoko, and the College of Science and Technology in Harper. There are several teacher-training colleges and a school for paramedics in Monrovia.

CHILD SOLDIERS

The UN estimates that 15,000 to 20,000 "child soldiers" under the age of 18 fought in Liberia's civil war, some even as young as six years old. Both boys and girls were recruited into the various armed groups and gangs.

The lack of electricity in homes has led students to use Monrovia's street lights to continue their studies after dark.

Medical supplies being sold in a market stall in Liberia.

The children were sometimes recruited by force—either they or their families were threatened with violence. At other times they joined out of necessity, because the soldiers had food or because they had become separated from their families amid the chaos of the civil war. Since the end of the civil war, most of these children have returned to civilian life, but many remain traumatized by their wartime experiences. One of the great challenges facing Liberia's new government is how to integrate these children back into society. International organizations such as the United Nations Children's Fund (UNICEF) have provided funding and training programs, where they can learn new skills as the first step to returning to living a normal life.

WELFARE

The welfare system, already overburdened and underfunded, was seriously shaken by the effects of war. The country currently has 120 doctors, while observers estimate that it needs at least 1,200 doctors to deal with postwar health care. The doctor-to-patient ratio was one to 50,000 in

2006. Liberia has just one medical college, from which 12 doctors graduate each year. Doctors and hospitals tend to be concentrated in the towns and cities. The most extensive health-care facilities are found in the Monrovia region and the industrial areas.

Many diseases that are fairly easy to eradicate elsewhere are endemic in Liberia, due to the disruptions caused by the war and other factors. Malaria is a serious problem. The disease is spread by mosquitoes, which breed in stagnant water. It can be tackled by treating mosquito breeding grounds and by taking medication once the disease is contracted. Both these tasks are difficult to undertake in a rainy country like Liberia, which has minimal infrastructure even in peacetime. Leprosy is a bacterial infection, but it is possible to make leprosy patients noninfectious with continuous medication. Liberia has leprosy centers where infected people can live and earn a living.

Smallpox and viral fever are diseases that can be prevented by immunization. They are less threatening in Liberia than they once were, but the disruption caused by the civil war has increased their incidence. Tuberculosis is another bacterial infection that has not been eradicated. Yaws, a skin infection, has been brought largely under control by a program conducted by the World Health Organization (WHO).

Poor-quality drinking water is a major problem in Liberia. Much of the nation's water is not safe for drinking, and this has led to an outbreak of diseases such as cholera, which, along with diarrhea, is one of the biggest

In the village of Gahtar, antimalarial tablets are distributed. Children and adults often swallow these with enthusiasm.

Every village has a palaver hut such as this one, where disputes are settled.

killers of children in the country. Unsafe drinking water can cause many diseases, the major killer being dysentery, which is caused by bacteria or parasites spread through contaminated food or water. Schistosomiasis is also caused by a parasite spread through unclean water, particularly river water. It kills slowly, destroying the internal organs, where the eggs of the parasite build up. Other major diseases in Liberia include trypanosomiasis, or sleeping sickness, intestinal worms, and elephantiasis.

Poor diet is an important factor in susceptibility to disease and, therefore, the high infant mortality rate. Measles, easily fought in developed countries, is another major contributor to infant mortality.

AIDS has also become a problem in Liberia, with an estimated 100,000 people living with the disease—approximately 3 percent of the population. The war has also left as many as 60 percent of Liberian women the victims of sexual violence, both physically and psychologically damaged.

TRIBAL AND VILLAGE LIFE

Given Liberia's several ethnic groups and ways of life, it is difficult to get an accurate picture of the typical village or community. Usually the villages are small. Often, but not always, they are ethnically homogenous, and the villagers' lifestyles are usually based on farming and hunting.

In the past Liberia was largely covered with dense forest, and people lived in small family units of a few huts in a clearing that they had hacked out for themselves. They grew a few crops and hunted and gathered the fruits of the forest. New areas of forest had to be cleared constantly, as the soil was not very fertile, and abandoned patches quickly returned to dense scrubland. Footpaths linked each family's clearing with those of their near relatives. Long journeys were hazardous and not undertaken lightly.

Modern villages are larger, but they are still made up of distantly related families. The village site is chosen for its good drainage, perhaps on high ground that can be defended easily, and near a stream for water—but not too close, since the spirits of the dead are believed to live in streams. Houses are circular huts built on a frame of poles. Through the poles are woven flexible branches, and plastered onto the branches is a fine mud collected from deserted termite nests. A conical roof extends over the house walls, forming a verandah. The roof tiles are split oil palm leaves.

Within each village is an open space for meetings and festivals, and a palaver hut where disputes are discussed and the village elders meet. It has a raised floor and palm-thatched roof but no walls, so that open meetings can be held there.

People from the smaller villages go to the larger ones on market day, usually to sell or shop.

Larger villages, often evolving along the roads built by foreign companies or along old trading routes, are more sophisticated. They have rectangular huts with corrugated iron roofs, and they hold a grand market day when people from the smaller villages congregate and the whole day is spent trading. Mandingo traders travel around the various village markets, which are intentionally held on different days.

Villages along the coast have a greater outside influence. The religions practiced there include Christianity, Islam, and native religions. Fishing is an important part of the economy. The Kru who live there build boats and catch fish to eat or sell. The women grow cassava, peanuts, and vegetables. Coastal people rely more on trade than do villagers in the interior.

THE FAMILY AND MARRIAGE

City dwellers in Liberia have Westernized attitudes toward marriage and the family. They believe in monogamous marriages, and their weddings sometimes include church services. The couple often meets at church or at a dance, and once the decision to marry has been made, they save money for their new home.

A modern bride arrives at the gate of her church.

Customs in the rural areas are quite different, as there are several forms of relationships between men and women, some that have an informal nature and others that involve serious bargaining between the two families and cash exchanges.

In traditional African society both children and wives are considered assets: Women can cook, work in the fields, look after children, and sell produce in the markets. Children, too, increase a man's wealth because of the future advantages they will give him—daughters can be sold for a bride price and sons help protect the group and can work in the fields. The children owe a debt to their parents, and the parents can call on their children for help in their old age.

Having more than one wife is legal, although fewer men are choosing to do this in modern Liberia because it is difficult to support a large family due to the economic problems facing postwar Liberia. Many men have at least two wives, each with her own hut, belongings, and children. In traditional Kpelle society it is the first wife who chooses the next one, often a friend or sister, perhaps one who is widowed. The first wife usually welcomes the help and company of another wife. There is no shame in being the second or third wife, and there is no legal distinction among the children of different wives. Very rich men have several wives and

BRIDE PRICE

In some tribal groups children are betrothed at a very young age in a contract arranged by both sets of parents. This usually involves the payment of bride price or "brideservice"—that is, work promised in lieu of payment. Very powerful men can offer political patronage as their bride price. Older men can afford to pay a bride price for their wife because they have savings or built-up wealth. This might be cash or livestock or even cloth, palm wine, nuts, or some other valuable object. Young men must offer some service to their future in-laws, such as work in their fields. Unless he is wealthy, at his marriage a man puts himself in debt to his in-laws for an indefinite period. If a man is very rich and powerful, people will be glad to give their daughters to him in return for his favors. Among the Kpelle, men like this are called *to nuu* (toh NEW), which the Kpelle translate as "big shot." Parents do not easily give up their daughters, since they represent potential wealth, and so there are many stories warning young girls about choosing the wrong husband.

children, and sometimes lend their wives to poorer men in exchange for their political support, manual labor, or some other favor.

Divorce is simple—a matter of arguing in front of the village elders over who gets what. Divorce is not a shameful affair. A man or woman who finds out that his or her partner is having an affair can get compensation for the loss of work or possessions that this represents. The extramarital relationship is not considered an immoral act, as it might be in Western society, but instead a threat to the economic structure of the family.

SECRET SOCIETIES

Most rural Liberians are members of some kind of secret society. Secret societies have a long history in Liberia, dating back to the 18th century. The two major ones are the Sande (SAN-day) and Poro (POH-roh), secret societies for women and men respectively. As people pass through the

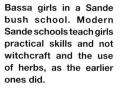

Bassa girls in a Sande bush school. Modern Sande schools teach girls practical skills and not witchcraft and the use of herbs, as the earlier ones did.

various stages in the society, they learn new rituals and lore that are mysteries to the uninitiated. Bush schools are held every year to induct young people. The Poro schools teach boys practical skills such as building liana (a type of tree) bridges, handling wives, and building houses, but they also teach tribal law, correct behavior toward elders, and secrets of religion. At one time endurance tests such as scarring were part of the course, though this is probably rare now. Elaborate festivals marked the start and end of the school.

The Sande schools used to teach girls cooking and the mysteries of marriage, childbirth, witchcraft, and the use of herbs, but now they are less magic-oriented and ritualistic and more cultural and practical.

There are some secret societies that are exclusive and, unlike the others, have a strong affiliation with the darker aspects of magic. The Leopard Society is one such group, now outlawed, whose members were said to have power over life and death. Another group is the Snake Society, whose rituals involve the handling of poisonous snakes.

The old, elite families had a powerful males-only secret society—the Ancient, Free, and Accepted Masonic Lodge of Liberia. The society was founded in 1867, and by 1980, when it was decimated in the coup, it had about 17 branches in Liberia. Virtually all of the nation's social and political leaders were members, and the lodge had a powerful influence on government decisions. The Masons were bitterly resented by the newly emerging young professionals of tribal origin in the 1970s and 1980s. There was also a women's version of the lodge—the Order of the Eastern Star of Africa.

The Masonic Temple is one of Monrovia's landmark buildings. Unfortunately, this was looted and burned in the 1980s coup.

RELIGION

SOME STATISTICS NAME Christianity as the most popular religion in Liberia, while others maintain that it is the least popular. What is certain is that there are three main faiths: Christianity, Islam, and traditional African religions. Statistics in 2007 suggested that 40 percent of Liberians classified themselves as Christian, 20 percent as Muslim, and 40 percent as holding indigenous, animist beliefs. These three faiths are not mutually exclusive. Some Liberians hold indigenous beliefs while at the same time maintaining a belief in either Christianity or Islam.

Christianity, the most recently introduced religion, was brought to Liberia by the early Americo-Liberian settlers and encouraged by missionary groups. Islam, both the Sunni and Shi'a sects, was introduced in West Africa by caravan merchants crossing the Sahara around the 11th century. Later it was spread by groups such as the Mandingo.

The oldest forms of religious belief in Liberia are the indigenous religions, of which animism is a common aspect. People who follow these religions believe in a supreme god, but spiritual power is usually experienced through everyday things or beings that are seen to be endowed with a supernatural element. Witchcraft is accepted by most people and is practiced regardless of religious conviction.

Above: **A statue of Christ stands before a Catholic church in Monrovia.**

Opposite: **Parishioners praying for peace in a cathedral in Liberia.**

TRIBAL RELIGIONS

Some official figures put animism as the religion of 90 percent of Liberia's population. Although the different groups' religious beliefs vary, the animistic religions of Liberia do have some features in common. Animists

believe in a spiritual world where things around them—trees, rocks, streams, virtually anything—are imbued with life and the power to cause harm or good. All objects encountered must therefore be treated with reverence. Objects can also be called upon to help the individual, usually through the aid of someone called a *zoe* (ZOH), the animist equivalent of a priest, doctor, and medium.

Animists believe in three gods—the creator, the ancestor, and the nature spirit. Of immediate importance to them are the latter two, which include different aspects of the spirit world.

Animists rely on the spirits of their ancestors to affect their own lives. The most recently deceased make the most powerful spirits. After death very important people are worshiped not only by their relatives but also by members of their village. As the generations pass the older spirits fade away into a group that is recognized in worship but not considered harmful.

A nature spirit is the spirit of a particular rock, tree, or river, which animists believe has the power to affect the lives of the people living near it. Animists give the object a name and try to appease it with sacrifices. A spirit may make an appearance in its true form, in which case viewers can be harmed or benefited, depending on how they treat it.

A practitioner of witch-craft sprinkles rice as she chants.

TOTEMISM

One aspect of the animistic religion can be seen in the Kpelle tribe. They practice a custom called totemism, where an individual has a special relationship with a particular object. This object represents a magical force that stands behind the individual (or, in some cases, the whole tribe) and guides and protects him or her. A totem might be a particular species of animal or plant, or even a rock. To the Kpelle each tribe's totem is the place where the ancestors reside. In the case of an individual, his or her totem might be a wildcat, a boar, or some other animal. Appearances of that animal can be taken as an omen. A father can pass his totem on to his son or a mother to her daughter. Most children are given a plant totem at birth. People with the same totem consider themselves to be kin, so a boy from one tribe whose totem is the leopard would feel kinship with another boy from a different tribe or village with the same totem.

MAGIC

Animists believe that the ancestral spirits and the spirits that reside in objects of nature can be used to bring about change. They appease these spirits

One possible reason why different figures are given for the various religious affiliations is that many tribal people hold two faiths: that of their tribal traditions and a new religion—Christianity or Islam.

The villagers' totems are kept in a totem hut.

through rituals and the offering of gifts. The practice is called magic or witchcraft, and the people who practice it are called magicians or medicine men.

These specialists, or *zoe*, are believed to be able to create medicine from herbs or animal tissue, which can be eaten, carried around as amulets, or hidden near people to affect them in a positive or negative way. Some of these are genuine herbal remedies, while others call on the belief of the people taking part in the magic to make it work. Sometimes the medicine calls for human flesh or organs.

Most urbanized Liberians claim that they no longer believe in magic, but there have been cases in recent history of powerful political figures using it. For instance, when President Samuel Doe was assassinated, he was left to die with his arms tied because of the belief of those who were around him that, if he were freed, his spirit would be released to gain power over another body.

CHRISTIANITY

The first Christians to arrive in Liberia were the American settlers. Their denominations were the Methodists and the Liberian Baptist Convention. The first director of the colony at Cape Mesurado, later renamed Monrovia, was Jehudi Ashmun, a Methodist minister. Methodism comes from the teachings of John Wesley, an 18th-century British Christian. Several separate black Methodist churches were formed, most of which disapproved of the attempt to resettle former slaves in Africa.

A medicine man displays his snakes.

Baptists belong to a Christian church that originated in England in the 17th century. Baptist churches are founded on the belief that the church is only for true believers, who must be baptized when they accept the belief and who must give testimony of their faith. There is no church hierarchy. A Baptist church is simple, as is its service. Baptists believe in the separation of church and state. Having said that, the ruling classes of Liberia were, for many years, mainly Baptists and Methodists. In the early days typical services in both churches were evangelical revival meetings, with singing and the giving of testimony. As time passed the services grew more subdued and formal.

The Catholic Church, the Lutheran Church, and the Episcopal Church arrived later. The Episcopal Church became a prestigious organization, adopted by many of the educated elite as well as educated Vai and tribal students at Cuttington University College. The Roman Catholic Church set up missions among the Kru, Grebo, and Krahn, and made many converts among those tribes. Lutherans have converted many of the Kpelle and Loma.

Sunday service in Saint Peter's Lutheran Church in a suburb of Monrovia. Soldiers of Samuel Doe's government massacred more than 600 civilians in this church in July 1990.

INDIGENOUS AFRICAN CHRISTIANITY

Over the years the mainstream churches with American origins have become less active and other Christian churches have emerged. Congregations of the newer churches tend to be ethnically homogeneous—that is, made up of only one tribe. The Liberian Assemblies of God, for example,

THE CHURCH OF THE LORD (ALADURA)

The Church of the Lord (Aladura) originated among the Yoruba people of Nigeria in the early 20th century. The name *Aladura* (AL-ad-ER-ah) means "Owners of Prayer." The church rejected both Western medicine and African traditional charms as agents of healing, and concentrated on the "laying on of hands" and prayer.

The Aladura Church began with a small group of Anglicans during an influenza epidemic in 1918, when many people were dying. It was inspired by American churches such as the Philadelphia Faith Tabernacle Church, which practiced faith healing. By the 1920s, when the Aladura was forced to leave the Anglican Church, it had become very popular.

By the 1960s the church had spread to Ghana, Togo, Liberia, Sierra Leone, and Benin. In Liberia it is a church of the town dwellers and is favored by city-dwelling Kpelle, Bassa, and Kru. Today there are several Aladura congregations in New York and London.

Some indigenous churches claim to have prophets who foretell the future and prepare amulets for spiritual protection. These amulets are inscriptions from the Bible, rather than herbs or animal bones.

has missions among the urban Kru. An indigenous African church, the Church of the Lord (Aladura), has faith healing, African music, and a lively atmosphere.

Members of the indigenous churches tend to be manual workers with little formal education, whereas members of mainstream churches are wealthy, literate, and often form politically powerful families.

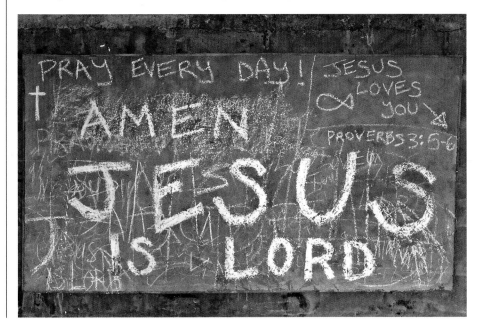

Christian graffiti at the lobby of the Docur Hotel in Monrovia.

ISLAM

Indigenous people have converted to Islam and Christianity in more or less equal numbers. Islam came to Liberia though the early caravan traders and was spread by the Mandingo, of whom around 90 percent profess Islam. The Vai have also converted to Islam in large numbers, as have other tribes, such as the Gola, Mende, Kissi, and Gbandi in the northwest.

Islam originated in Arabia in the seventh century, following the teachings of the Prophet Muhammad. Muslims believe in one God, in angels who bring his word to the people, and in the 28 prophets who received God's message. One of those prophets, they believe, was Jesus Christ. Others include Abraham, David, Moses, and the writers of the New Testament, all figures known in Christianity. Muslims also believe in a final day of judgment, when they will hear the sound of the angel Asrafil blowing a trumpet. There are five pillars of Islam, or things a Muslim must do: declaration of the one true God with Muhammad as his prophet, prayer, fasting, making a pilgrimage to Mecca, and giving alms to the poor.

The form of Islam practiced in Liberia is largely Sunni, or orthodox Islam. The Sunnis acknowledge the first four caliphs as the rightful successors of the Prophet Muhammad. The Lebanese community in Liberia consists of Shi'a Muslims. Shi'as believe Muhammad was succeeded by his son-in-law, Ali, and that Ali will one day return. A small number of Liberian Muslims profess Ahmadiya Islam, a heretical form not considered to be the true faith by other sects.

The Mandingo mosque in Gbarnga. Islam was spread throughout Liberia by the Mandingo, who were traditionally traveling traders.

LANGUAGE

LIBERIA HAS AN EXTREMELY complex system of languages. Its indigenous languages can be divided into three main groups, all belonging to the Niger-Congo group of languages: the West Atlantic or Mel, Kwa, and Mande, the last of which is the most popular, spoken by more than a million people. The Niger-Congo languages account for 1,000 languages in sub-Saharan Africa. In addition, there is the official language, which is English, and various forms of "pidgin English" that are spoken around the country.

The three main language groups consist of more than 30 subgroups and dialects. Some groups, such as the Vai, have also adopted Arabic. This makes communication quite a problem. Intertribal communication is often made through a common root language or pidgin English. It is common for Liberians to be multilingual.

It is thought that the Kru, considered to be good sailors, have given their name to the English word for men who work on a ship—crew.

Left: **Newspapers being sold in Liberia. There are more than 30 languages and dialects in Liberia, but English is the main language of communication in the towns.**

Opposite: **Liberian refugees reading books.**

In Weasua, a small town in the northwest of Grand Cape Mount County, it is claimed that you can hear every indigenous Liberian language spoken.

ENGLISH

English is the official government language and the language of education. It is the mother tongue of about 2.5 percent of Liberia's population, but it is spoken in one form or another as a second language by at least half of the population. It differs sharply from the other forms of African English in that it uses American word choices. For example, the terms used in reference to the secondary school system are *high school, junior high school, grades, vacation, graduation*—rather than the British English terms used in some other African countries. In Nigeria you buy "biscuits" in a "shop," whereas in Liberia you buy "cookies" in a "store." Indigenous African names are becoming more common, but European first and last names have long been accepted as normal. This tradition goes back to the freed slaves who brought non-African names with them. Indeed every one of Liberia's presidents had or has a European last name.

Right: **Peace demonstrators carrying English language boards. English is widely spoken and understood in Liberia, particularly in the urban areas.**

Opposite: **In addition to standard American English, many other pidgin forms exist in Liberia.**

In addition to the standard American English of broadcasting, government, the courts, and international business, there are many pidgin forms. The English language came to Liberia with the Americo-Liberians, many of whom spoke an African-American Creole form of English when they arrived. This evolved into an amalgamation much closer to the indigenous languages than, say, the Krio pidgin language of neighboring Sierra Leone, which had only one wave of pidginization. In Monrovia there are many pidgins, each one influenced by the mother tongue of the tribe. In some cases—for example, the Monrovian pidgin called Kepama—the pidgin has become the mother tongue and is spoken more easily than the original language.

BIG SHOTS

The various tribes of Liberia had a social structure that respected a certain number of wealthy men who grew very powerful within tribal groups, had many wives, and could call on several men for assistance during conflicts with other groups. When people with these customs came into contact with English-speaking people, the nearest translation for such a person was "big shot." In English *big shot* is almost a term of abuse to describe someone who shows off wealth, but it does not have that connotation in Liberian English.

The Americo-Liberians fit in with the indigenous people's idea of what a big shot was and so they were given the kind of respect reserved for tribal leaders. Big shots were expected to show off their wealth and use it for political purposes. After the coup in the 1980s many big shots fell out of favor with the new regime and were killed, and it became less socially acceptable, if not positively dangerous, to be a big shot, because it represented a challenge to the government of the day, led by Samuel Doe.

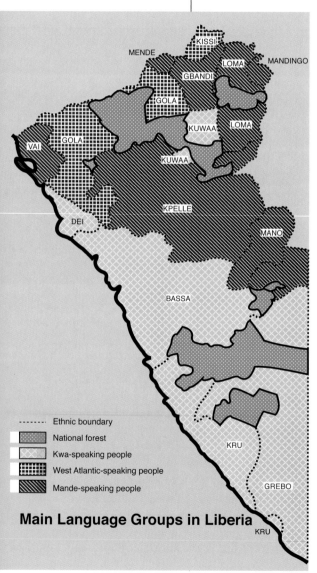

Main Language Groups in Liberia

Legend:
- - - - - Ethnic boundary
- National forest
- Kwa-speaking people
- West Atlantic-speaking people
- Mande-speaking people

Map labels: KISSI, MENDE, LOMA, MANDINGO, GBANDI, GOLA, KUWAA, LOMA, VAI, GOLA, KUWAA, KPELLE, DEI, MANO, BASSA, KRU, GREBO, KRU

REGIONAL LANGUAGES

The Mande languages are not restricted to Liberia. They extend into Mali, Guinea, the Ivory Coast, and Sierra Leone. In Liberia they are spoken by the Vai, Mandingo, Gbandi, Kpelle, Loma, Mende, Gio, and Mano. Most Mande speakers live in the north and east, with only the Vai living on the coast. Not all Mande speakers can understand one another.

There are many variations of the Kwa language, most of them not spoken in Liberia. They are spoken by the Bassa (the largest ethnic group in Monrovia), Kru, Dei, Bella, Krahn, Kuwaa, and Grebo. Kwa speakers inhabit the coastline and the south of the country. Typical of the Kwa languages is the use of tones to give context to a word. The closeness of Kwa languages can be seen in the word for "water," which is *ni* (NEE) in Bassa, Kru, and Kuwaa. Similarly the word for "tree" is *chu* (CHU) in all three languages.

The West Atlantic speakers are the Gola and Kissi of Liberia and Sierra Leone. These tribes, the oldest inhabitants of Liberia, live in the north. Their languages form part of a group of 23 spoken around West Africa, the most important of which is Fulani. Like Chinese these languages use tones to indicate meaning.

LINGUA FRANCAS

The main intertribal language is pidgin English, but there are also several tribal languages at a local level.

For example, in northern and western Liberia, all three of the main language groups exist in close proximity. Most people speak their own language and at least one of the other two language families. As long as three people are speaking, they can be mutually understood.

In regions like this—particularly the area northwest of Monrovia—some indigenous languages are disappearing as the people adopt not English, but one of the other native languages. The Dei, for example, have taken up the Vai language at home as well as in business. Malinke (mah-LINK-ee), the language spoken by the Mandingo, has become a lingua franca or common language, because of the Mandingo's traditional role as traveling traders.

In some unusual cases the speakers of one language can understand another language but cannot be understood by speakers of the other language. For example, the Gbee speakers of Nimba County can understand the language of the Bassa but cannot be understood by them.

English is the language of choice for educated Liberians, and it is used in politics, newspapers, and in radio and television broadcasts.

ACCENTS AND DIFFERENT MEANINGS

Although it is acknowledged that Liberians speak a form of American English, American *kwi* (KWEE, pidgin for "foreigners") in Monrovia would have a hard time understanding what the person on the street was saying, though the former would be clearly understood. Many of the final sounds of words are not pronounced, and a great many others are slurred. There are also some differences in usage that might be confusing. For example, many words have the suffix "o," so "cheap" becomes "cheap-o." Buses, cars, motorbikes—in fact, any wheeled vehicle—are all called a "car." The word *palaver* is commonly used to mean a "discussion," while in English it means "a lot of fuss about nothing." If you want to congratulate someone, you must say "thank you!"

Above: **Schoolchildren in towns receive instruction in English.**

Bottom: **Vai script. The Vai were the first people in Liberia to invent a usable written language.**

WRITTEN LANGUAGES

In many cases the first written form of any African language came about through the efforts of missionaries, particularly Lutherans, who created a written form so that they could teach the Bible to the tribes. In Liberia this was not the case. The vast number of subdialects made the work of the missionaries very difficult, since what might be understandable to one group would make no sense to people in a neighboring village.

A script was developed for the Kpelle, and alphabets were created for some other languages, but the first usable written language was invented by the Vai for their language. In the early 19th century a Vai named Dualu Bukele developed a script for their language. It came into common use and became the basis for written versions of other languages. The script is not an alphabet but rather a syllabary. It has about 240 characters, each standing for a different vowel/consonant combination. Originally used to keep records of births, deaths, and marriages, and never used by women, the script is now used only by elderly men and is passed on to interested scholars. It was never taught in schools. Before the introduction of English, the Vai script was used by the Loma, Kpelle, and Mende in their record keeping. During World War II German intelligence officers used the Vai script to pass coded messages.

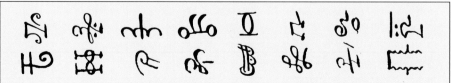

OTHER INFLUENCES

Early explorers of the region included the Portuguese, who gave names to some of Liberia's geographic features. The Mesurado River, for example, was named by the Portuguese and means "measured" or "quiet," probably because the mouth of the river is calm. The Gallinas River has a Portuguese name that means "hens."

The names of the Saint John and Saint Paul rivers have been anglicized, but they were originally Portuguese names. The name of the Cess River comes from the Portuguese word *cestor*, meaning "basket" (probably after the basket-wielding fisherwomen the explorers saw there). The Sanguin River got its name because it runs red during a flood (*sanguin* is Portuguese for "red"), and the Cavalla River got its name because it has plenty of mackerel ("mackerel" is *caballa* in Portuguese). The name for the region of Liberia bordering on the Gulf of Guinea—the Grain Coast—also comes from the Portuguese, who named it for the grains of melegueta pepper they found growing there.

Liberian proverbs teach truths by relating to daily life: "He who steps in first shows the depth of the current" means that it is wise to stay back and watch others before acting, since what happens to them can teach one what to do. "One does not throw a stick after the snake has gone" is advice that means to seize opportunity when it occurs.

TALKING DRUMS

Common throughout West Africa, the talking drums were an early form of communication in Liberia. They are shaped like an hourglass, with skins covering both ends. The skins are connected by tightly stretched rawhide cords. The expert drum player can alter the sound of the drum by stretching or releasing these chords, thus creating a series of tones similar to the tonal languages of Liberia.

The drummers learned a set series of beats and tones, which became a kind of Morse code that corresponded to the pattern of the actual words. A talking-drum player made the music his life's work. The sound of the drums carried over long distances, and messages could be relayed over hundreds of miles in a very short time.

ARTS

IN TRADITIONAL LIBERIAN CULTURE the arts, leisure, religion, and festivals coincide in the colorful pageants and festivals of village life. In modern Liberian society the arts include literature and music, with both tribal and Western influences. Unfortunately two decades of civil war have destroyed much of Liberia's material culture, including many priceless artifacts and rare works of art.

LITERATURE

Traditional literature arrived in Liberia with the ancestors of the Kpelle and Kru as they migrated across Africa from Sudan. They brought with them stories, parables, and proverbs, as well as legends about their ancestors' lives. The oral tradition was passed down by the fireside, in the bush schools, and in the meeting place of the village, where festivals celebrating the ancient stories were held. Although most tribes had no written form of language, the stories survived, but each time they were told they were altered a little, or some new ideas were added, so the stories grew in the telling.

One example of an ancient story is the Woi epic, which is told by a professional storyteller. Every storyteller has his or her own way of telling it, but the basic sequence of events is the same. If everyone is having a good time, the Woi epic storytelling session may extend beyond just one evening. Many events in the tale are comic, and current events are often drafted into the story to give it a topical element.

In modern times anthropologists have recorded many of the oral stories, but as tribal living gradually gives way to an urban lifestyle the stories will fade away and lose their usefulness.

Above: **A potter from the Kpelle tribe shapes and decorates his clay pots.**

Opposite: **A woman from the Kpelle tribe weaving a traditional bag.**

AMERICO-LIBERIAN LITERATURE

The saying "There is no wealth where there are no children" shows the great value put on family life in Liberia. The proverb "If you marry a beautiful wife you marry trouble" advises young Liberians to look beyond appearances when choosing a wife.

When the freed slaves sailed to Africa and settled in Liberia, they brought with them a complex cultural system. When their ancestors were taken to the United States or the Caribbean, they were separated from others who spoke their language and knew their stories. The chances of their being with others from their own tribe were low. So they learned a common language, and the stories they brought with them from America became amalgamated into a new culture, intermingled with the adopted culture of their new home in Liberia. The people who settled in Liberia in the early 19th century had a culture that included 200 years of remembered African culture and was largely Christian, democratic, and literate.

The new settlers could read and write, and they had as their literary background the hymns and religious texts of Christianity. Their early literary efforts were a reaction to their pioneering status. Their lives were hard: They were trying to make a new and better life for themselves, but they discovered a country where African people traded slaves, where there was constant intertribal warfare, and where survival demanded a fight against the elements. The literary products of this were religious poetry and collected pulpit narrations, all with the common theme of the people's need to rely on God to see them through the difficult times.

With the two cultures—Americo-Liberian and African—gradually assimilating ideas from one another, a new Liberian literature has emerged, which parallels the emergence of black literature in English across Africa. A journal called *Kaafa* (KAH-feh) publishes short stories by Liberian writers, while, for a time, a Liberian publisher called Liberian Literary and Educational Publications was active in Monrovia.

Liberia's best-known novel is *Murder in the Cassava Patch*, by Bai T. Moore (1916–88), published in 1968. It is a novel about forbidden relationships and taboos, and is required reading for Liberian students. Some successful writers of the last few decades include Robert Brown, a lecturer at the University of Liberia, who has written novels and short stories; Elizabeth Mitchel, a writer of essays and short stories as well as a short novel; R. Sylvanus Corker, who writes short stories and worked in the Liberian embassy in Washington; and Wilton G. S. Sankawulo, a novelist and short-story writer who was briefly chair of the Council of State.

The first Liberian novel was called Love in Ebony *and was written by Charles Cooper in the late 19th century.*

AN 1836 POEM

Here is part of a poem by Americo-Liberian Hilary Teague, written in 1836:

> We sing the wondrous deeds of Him
> Who rides upon the sky;
> His name is God, the glorious theme
> Is sung by saints on high.

After a few stanzas praising God, she gets down to the story she has to tell:

> We were by those beset around,
> Who craved to drink our blood,
> Whose malice, hatred knew no bound,
> Whose hearts of love were void.
>
> The savage yell, the dreadful cry,
> Fell on our frightened ear,
> The gleaming spear, the clam'ring throng,
> With terror did appear.

The poem carries on in a similar vein and style, with God eventually calming the savages. It is written in the language of 19th-century hymns—for example, "We were by those beset around." The poem gives some idea of the reaction of the settlers to what must have been a frightening savagery around them.

FOLKTALES

Common throughout Africa are spider stories, and Liberia has its own versions of these: Ananse (ah-NAN-say) the spider is a clever trickster, but his cleverness often brings about the wrong result, and he usually gets caught in the end. The spider stories found their way into American culture by way of the slaves brought from Africa.

Another set of stories kept alive in the oral tradition includes legends about ancestors. These stories probably began at the funeral of some great leader, where those at the celebration would improvise and probably exaggerate the stories of battles fought or animals killed. If the stories were good, bits would be remembered and repeated at the next celebration, and so on. Proverbs were another part of the oral tradition and were used to pass on the culture and values of the tribe.

ARCHITECTURE

Each tribe has its own version of private houses and meetinghouses. The secret societies also build places for their meetings. Sande meeting places are plain, while Poro huts are elaborately decorated. Ordinary houses are painted in geometric designs by women and pictorial designs by men. Kpelle houses are, by tradition, rectangular, with their outer walls decorated and a little covered porch area in one corner. Gio huts are circular, with a high mud platform around the base, into which the roof supports are embedded. Bassa huts are rectangular, with a long porch along the front.

Folktales are handed down at informal gatherings, such as this group of Gio's villagers.

100

THE GREEDY SPIDER

This story of Ananse the spider is told to Liberian children to warn them about the dangers of greed.

Ananse was invited to two village feasts, but he feared that if he went to one he would miss the other. So he tied two pieces of rope around his body and told each village chief to pull on the rope when his feast was ready. That way he could be there for both feasts. But it so happened that both feasts began at the same time. Each village elder pulled the rope from his village to call Ananse. Ananse, who had been sleeping under a tree between the two villages, could not move. One rope pulled him one way, and the other rope pulled him the other way. When he did not arrive at either village, the chiefs began to pull harder. Ananse felt himself being pulled apart. When the feasts were over, the chiefs set out to find out what had happened to Ananse. They found him nearly dead. They untied the ropes, and Ananse was so ashamed of his greediness that he ran away and hid.

The settlers built houses based on the style of 19th-century houses from Virginia and the Carolinas. Consequently public buildings of the early period were Georgian in style, while in the 1920s a kind of Afro-Brazilian style became popular. In the 1950s, during an economic upturn, many public buildings were designed by European architects in a modern style. Under the rule of Samuel Doe some very grand marble and glass buildings were erected.

Young women stand on the porch of a house with simply decorated whitewashed walls in Belefenai.

The National Culture Center in Kendeja displays the architecture of 16 ethnic groups from Liberia.

MUSIC

Music is an important part of daily life in Liberia and a vibrant expression of Liberian culture. In tribal society rhythm is a basic accompaniment to most activities—rowing boats, sowing seeds, cutting plants, and building houses. Funerals, births, and war all call for different songs. Today the gospel music of the churches fills the airwaves, and collections of traditional songs have been modernized.

Traditional music has a distinctive sound because of the instruments used. Various types of xylophone are common, often with gourds hanging below them to create a resonance. Rattles of all kinds—made out of anything from gourds to tin cans—are also used, as well as various stringed instruments. These might be simple lutes—made from a gourd with simple strings—or, in modern times, acoustic guitars. Bells,

A typical Vai musical ensemble. Music is an essential component of life in Liberia, both rural and urban.

clappers, horns, and, of course, drums make up the orchestra. The most important element of Liberian music is rhythm rather than melody. As in all West African music, drums and other percussion instruments are used to set up complex beat patterns, with different rhythms overlaying one another.

Modern Liberian music has borrowed from this tradition and also from the "Highlife" big-band music of Ghana and Sierra Leone, a dance style that emerged in the 1950s using African rhythms alongside regimental band music, Latin American rhythms, and calypso music. As soon as recording became possible in Liberia in the 1920s collections of Liberian music began to feature a female Vai singer named Zondogbo. Later, during World War II, there were many Americans stationed in Liberia; their music came with them and influenced local styles.

Traditional music was at its most vibrant in the 1960s, when singers such as Zuke Kiazolu and Zina Zaldoa were recorded. Two radio stations, ELBC and ELWA, broadcast popular songs daily and sent researchers out to the rural areas to collect new folk songs.

In modern Liberia, Americo-Liberian music is largely gospel-style. Popular music has suffered the effects of the civil war. Local music is available only on bootleg cassette tapes and is either linked with American soul/funk music, as in the music of Dave or Big Steve Warjloh, or is more West African in style, as in the music Gbesa Body, who plays folk guitar. Molly Dorley is famous for having led the movement for the creation of a national Liberian identity through her songs.

A Gio man plays one of Liberia's many traditional stringed instruments.

The Kru are famous for their choirs that sing in a complex series of harmonies.

Masks are far more than decorative objects—in the Sande and Poro cults, especially, they are believed to be the embodiment of the power they represent. Many such masks were collected in the middle of the 20th century by anthropologists.

A LIVING ART AND CRAFT

Art is a part of everyday life in Liberia. Elaborate masks and colorful costumes are made for tribal festivals and religious rituals. Although they are considered sacred objects, the masks have been given away to anthropologists—in an effort to preserve them—by tribal leaders who saw their traditions being lost in the move to Westernize Liberian society.

The masks are made of sapwood and often have steel or aluminum teeth. They are usually brightly painted with dyes collected from indigenous plants and can be beautiful or fierce-looking, depending on their purpose. One type of mask has an elongated beak, while another has tubular protruding eyes and a horn on its forehead.

Today replicas of these masks are made for cultural purposes and as craft objects. Woodcarvers make figures from ebony, camwood, cherry, walnut, and mahogany. The Kissi carve figures from soapstone, while the Grebo make clay models. Dan artists cast jewelry in bronze or brass using the lost wax method.

Before the civil war modern art flourished in Monrovia, with galleries displaying the paintings and sculptures of local artists. The National Museum was looted during the civil war, but a collection of masks and ceramics survives at the Cuttington University College.

Among the America-Liberian community, painting and sculpture only began in the mid-20th century, and the arts were largely religious in nature. In the 1960s a Liberian school of artists emerged, many of them having been trained in Europe, and by the 1970s regular exhibitions were being held. After the 1990 coup two prominent artists, Jallah Kollie and Vanjah Richards, were killed, and a third, Cietta Mensah, left Liberia for the United States. Richards, a sculptor and painter, was commissioned before the coup to paint scenes of Liberian history and mythology for several large hotels and public buildings. Painters who have remained in Liberia and survived the fighting include Wantue Major, who focuses on graphic images of the horror of war; Omar al Shabu; and Winston Richards, an abstract expressionist.

Craftwork from Liberia includes masks, figures carved from wood and ivory in designs taken from the totems of indigenous religions, woven mats and baskets, cloth, gold and silver jewelry, and musical instruments. Dru, a woodcarver from Liberia, has found fame with exhibitions of his work in the United States.

When the Carthaginian explorer Hanno landed on what is thought to be Liberian soil in the fifth century B.C., he recorded that he and his men spent a sleepless night listening to the sound of drumming coming from the jungle around them. It convinced them to leave the next morning.

The *sowei* (SOH-way) or *zogbei* (Zog-bay), a mask in the shape of a helmet that covers the entire head, is used in Sande rituals. It is unique in that it is the only mask used and owned solely by women.

LEISURE

BEFORE THE CIVIL WAR drove expatriate workers out of Liberia and sent half of the population into refugee camps outside the nation's borders, leisure activities in the country could be classified into three main types. In the cities there were a variety of urban leisure facilities, such as movie theaters, art galleries, clubs, discos, and sporting facilities and events, some of which have survived the war. Films continue to be very popular, with about 1.5 million people going to the movies every year. In the inner city of Monrovia and in the mining and agricultural concessions run by foreign companies, there were clubs, restaurants, and sporting facilities for the expatriate workers. In the rural areas, in the long post-harvest period, villagers had the time and money to relax and enjoy the dancing and singing during their numerous festivals. At other times they enjoyed just relaxing in a hammock under the trees.

Left: **In the towns, both Western and African styles of dancing are in vogue, but in the villages traditional rhythms are favored.**

Opposite: **Boys enjoying a game of checkers.**

The markets in small towns are different from those in the cities, with unusual animals being sold for food and medicine, as well as herbs collected in the forest, charms, and talismans.

LEISURE IN THE CITIES

Monrovia is a small and poor city by the standards of the developed world. It has been left considerably damaged by the fighting and disruption of the last 20 years. However, in times of relative peace, its citizens can choose from a range of leisure pursuits. There are movie theaters, although there is no Liberian film industry. Chinese kung-fu films are very popular. There are cafés, known locally as cookshops, where simple Liberian food can be eaten, as well as more upscale restaurants for an evening out. Clubs and discos, a few with satellite TV and some with live music, have a charged atmosphere. Churchgoers often have their own organized functions, and the tribal associations also have meeting places and organized activities. Markets are a popular leisure spot for people who shop daily for groceries, household goods, and cloth. There are a few Western-style supermarkets that mainly sell imported foods.

In the smaller towns there are frequent power cuts, so evening diversions are limited to the nights when there is electricity.

RURAL LEISURE ACTIVITIES

Rural life in Liberia consists of work, leisure, festivals, and the arts. Until the harvest most people have little time for leisure pursuits, but when the harvest is over many men plan a hunting trip, partly for food and partly for the pleasure of the hunt. Pipe smoking is a popular way of relaxing for both men and women. So is drinking palm wine in the evenings, with a kola nut as a chaser. A popular leisure game played all over Africa is called *mancala* (man-KAH-lah). It is a little like checkers and is played on a two- to three-foot wooden boat-shaped board with hollows for the counters.

Liberians love to talk wherever they are, whether in the workplace and at the fireside. They have a long tradition of recording their history and beliefs in epic tales that help pass on their values to succeeding generations. These values are evident even on informal family evenings, when conversations are peppered with stories, proverbs, and cautionary tales.

Two Dan villagers enjoy a quiet game of *mancala*. The objective is to go around the board, taking as many of the opponent's counters as possible while protecting one's own.

LEISURE FOR EXPATRIATES

Most foreigners in Liberia were evacuated by their governments in 1990. Since Johnson-Sirleaf's election victory in 2005, some have ventured back into the country, but the large expatriate workforce has yet to return. When there were expatriates in the country, their leisure needs were catered to by clubs, TV bars, private swimming pools, and expensive restaurants. Yekepa, the second-largest town in Liberia, is a big iron concession town. Before the civil war it doubled as a highland resort for wealthy Liberians and expatriates. The town has many sports facilities, including an Olympic-sized swimming pool and a golf course, the only one in the world that straddles two countries (Liberia and Guinea).

SPORTS

The most popular sport in Liberia is association soccer. An intercounty competition is held for the national championship every year. Local teams

Prior to the civil war, expatriates in Monrovia frequented the Hotel Africa, with its lawns, swimming pool, and up-scale restaurants.

play in a national association, and Liberia plays in an African league. Liberia has occasionally qualified for the African Cup of Nations without having ventured beyond the first round, but has never qualified for the soccer World Cup.

Other sports that are popular, particularly in the cities, include basketball, swimming, and squash, although swimming pools and squash courts tend to be found mostly in expatriate clubs. Liberia has a national basketball team. Schoolchildren enjoy playing kickball, which is played on the same diamond-shaped court as baseball, with a pitcher and home runs, but the ball is kicked rather than hit with a bat. Another children's game is like marbles, often played with dried seeds. Four marbles (or seeds) are stacked in a pyramid on the ground, and players flick their own marbles toward it in order to knock it down. The first to do so wins the marbles.

Boys being taught soccer in Liberia. Soccer is the most popular sport in the country.

A Liberian man listening to the news on a transistor radio.

THE MEDIA

In the city there is electricity for most of the day and television is watched for a few hours daily. Television has not yet become a major part of people's lives, chiefly because of the expense of the equipment. Liberia's state-run Liberian Broadcasting System (LBS) has no television service, and is struggling to maintain a single radio service. Radios are more widely used, and there are several radio stations picked up from outside Liberia, including Voice of America. The BBC World Service as well as a Sudanese station can be picked up in Liberia. Until 1990 there were many local newspapers, but since then there has been tight press control. Few foreign newspapers are available. Four dailies are published in Liberia, although they are small because of the damage in Monrovia—*Inquirer*, *Daily Observer*, *The Analyst*, and *Monrovia Daily News*. A regional journal called *West Africa Magazine* was banned in Liberia from 1985 to 1990 because of its criticism of the government. Internet use is not yet very popular in Liberia because of the legacy of the civil war, and few people can access the Internet from their homes.

GAMES AND SONGS

Villagers enliven many of their activities with song. Cradle songs are an example of the use of music in daily life. Songs also come into play in children's games. Among the Gola there is a game called *nenya* (NEN-

Liberian children singing along as one of them sets the beat with a drum.

yah). A group of children choose one child to pretend to be a grain of rice. Another child must protect the grain of rice from the other children, who are all hungry birds. The children must creep into the circle drawn around the "rice" and tag it without being tagged themselves. A tagged "bird" becomes the "rice." As they dart in and out of the circle, the children sing a song that mimics the call of the birds in the fields.

An all-boys game played by Vai children is *Mba N Ko Dende* (MBAR ehn koh DEN-de), or "Mother Give Me a Canoe." All the children hold hands in a circle and choose one boy to be "it." He has to find a weak spot in the chain of hands and break it. As he does so he sings a song about canoes, asking if he can take the canoe. If a child in the chain answers "yes," the boy who is "it" can try to break his hold. When he succeeds, the next boy enters the circle and the game begins again.

Children also play games similar to tag. One is known as the crab game. A line is drawn on the ground, and two teams line up along it with their hands and feet on the ground behind them a little like crabs. Only their feet are allowed to cross the line. The object is to tag one of their opponents with the foot before the opponent tags them. Those who are tagged must sit out of the game.

FESTIVALS

FESTIVALS IN LIBERIA ARE DOMINATED by the three main religions practiced—Christianity, Islam, and animism. All have changed as they have come in contact with one another. Christian festivals, for example, have taken on a more energetic style common to local religious practices, with drumming and colorful processions. With the spread of Islam and Christianity, local festivals are taking on a less dominant role in village society.

Falling somewhere between entertainment and festival are the many vibrant song, dance, and performance events that take place in the rural areas. The Kpelle call these events *pelee* (PEL-ee). Sande and Poro festivals also include vigorous celebration, dance, and other activities.

In the last decade or so of war, much of Liberian culture, including festivals, was disrupted to the point of extinction. Peace has now returned to the country, and the traditional celebrations are being revived.

In a daily ceremony, the national flag is raised at 7:45 A.M. at every school.

Left: **Christian festivals in Liberia may include staged performances.**

Opposite: **A fire dancer performing in Ganta, northern Liberia, during a festival.**

Above: **Women performing a dance during Christmas in Liberia. Christmas is celebrated with enthusiasm, even in the rural areas, as it coincides with the long period of leisure and celebration among villagers when the harvest is over and people have money.**

Opposite: **A man beats his drum during the Bassa farming festival, which takes place in February, when the new crops are about to be sown.**

The North American celebration of Thanksgiving, a public holiday in Liberia, is a time for families to get together.

CHRISTIAN FESTIVALS

Liberian Christians celebrate the main Christian festivals, and Christmas and Easter are public holidays. There are Christian missions in every small town that celebrate the festivals with a mixture of African and Christian traditions. African churches such as the Aladura celebrate with colorful processions, music with a lively rhythm, and emotionally charged services involving miracle events such as talking in tongues and faith healing. The older Baptist churches are more sedate. At Christmas, gifts are given and church bells are rung. Easter is a more somber occasion, since it marks the crucifixion, resurrection, and assumption of Christ.

MUSLIM FESTIVALS

Muslim festivals are not public holidays in Liberia, but they are celebrated throughout the country. Because the Muslim calendar is based on the moon's revolution around the Earth rather than the Earth's revolution around the Sun, the dates of Muslim festivals change every year. Ramadan, the ninth month of the Islamic calendar, is a period of fasting that lasts from dawn to dusk. In the evenings the fast is broken, and in Muslim areas the cookshops stay open and there is an atmosphere of celebration. Eid al-Fitr, the festival that marks the end of Ramadan, lasts four days from the first day of the 10th month. The family home is cleaned and new clothes are bought. Families visit one another, and great feasts are held. For Muslims this celebrates the successful end of a period of spiritual cleansing and is the most important event of the year. Eid al-Adha, the 10th day of the 12th month, celebrates Abraham's willingness to sacrifice his son. An animal is slaughtered, and meat is given to the poor.

AFRICAN FESTIVALS

Many African festivals take place in the fall, when the hard work of the year is over and the harvest is gathered. The Sande and Poro festivals often take place then, and the proper celebration of events such as funerals is delayed until this time, when suitable attention can be paid to them.

The Go Ge (go GAY) is one ritual with roots in the ancient ways of village life. When a particularly disruptive dispute occurred in a village, someone would be called in to arbitrate. This was the Go Ge, often the village leader wearing a disguising mask. The term is roughly translated as "Cow Devil." The Go Ge would arrive ceremoniously and mediate between the warring parties. At the resolution of the problem, a cow would be sacrificed by the loser and a feast would be held.

THE WOI EPIC

Festivals are often an occasion for bringing the professional storyteller into the village for a performance involving music, storytelling, dance, and mime. The stories are often epic poems that exist only in the memories of the storytellers.

One well-recorded example of this is a Kpelle myth called the Woi epic, a complicated story about a superhuman hero called Woi. Ananse the naughty spider is in the story, as are several objects that are personified, such as Woi's house, bow, ax, and cutlass. Woi's bull has been stolen by the Yele Lawo, a monster spirit, and Woi has to go to battle to retrieve it. Many adventures and fights beset Woi and his allies as he tries to move his house into the sky.

The storyteller organizes a chorus that sings in between episodes of the story. When is the chorus has been trained, he turns to persons in the audience and makes them the questioners, or *mar kee ke nuu* (mar KEY kay new). They call out questions about the events, to give the storyteller the links to the next part of the story and provide feedback that everyone understands. Finally the whole audience is organized into sections, all singing or chanting or playing (tapping on drums and bottles) at different rhythms at the same time. If a section of the audience makes a mistake, the storyteller can call on another section and get the rhythm and story going again.

As he tells the story the storyteller sits up on his knees, using his arms as a shadow play of events, the lanterns and torches around him creating a larger-than-life figure. The story has no beginning and no end. The storyteller can begin with an episode that suits the evening's performance, and he carries on until all the episodes are told. It is unlikely that this epic is written down anywhere or even recorded, and so as the older generation dies out and the younger people go off to the towns, chances are that Woi's epic will be lost for all time.

WEDDINGS

Most tribal weddings are grand celebrations, with performances by special dance troupes, a great feast, and gift giving. These ceremonies often end with a procession of the newlyweds and their friends to the groom's village.

Among the Kpelle, however, weddings are a very low-key, if not quite secret, business. What is important in Kpelle weddings is the acknowledgment by the head of the family that the union is official. A Kpelle wedding involves the tribal elders giving the newlyweds advice about marital responsibilities. The couple's relatives attend and must give assurances that they will intervene in any marital disputes. A small token is given by the groom's relatives to the bride's, and the woman is ceremoniously handed over to the man. Bride wealth negotiations are settled, and then the ritual is over.

Africa Day (May 25) celebrates the people and cultures of the African continent. It is celebrated in all African countries and other places in the world where African people live.

CALENDAR OF PUBLIC HOLIDAYS

January 1	New Year's Day
February 11	Armed Forces Day
Second Wednesday in March	Decoration Day
March 15	J. J. Roberts's Birthday
April 11	National Redemption Day
Second Friday in April	Prayer and Fast Day
Variable	Good Friday
Variable	Easter Sunday
May 14	National Unification Day
May 25	Africa Day
July 26	National Independence Day
First Thursday in November	Thanksgiving Day
November 29	William Tubman's Birthday
December 25	Christmas

A Bassa girl in Rivercess County with the traditional body paint of a Sande initiate.

SECRET SOCIETY FESTIVALS

Secret societies are not important in modern urban life, but in rural areas it is still customary for most young men and women to undergo a period of instruction in bush schools; when they emerge they are considered adults. This event now lasts only a few weeks, to fit in with the school term, but in the past it lasted a few years. All boys and girls of a certain age are inducted into the secret society in a ceremony that symbolizes the death of the old person. The rituals involved in the Sande and Poro ceremonies are rites of passage from childhood to adulthood. The masks and costumes of each society are kept in the society hut and may not be seen by outsiders. They completely cover the wearer, who is often the highest-ranking member of the society. In one Poro ceremony each boy is completely swallowed up by the masked figure, who wears a huge straw costume. This signifies the death of the boy. Other rituals act out the impaling of the boy. When he returns to his family he is supposed to be a different person.

Another ritual, called "breaking the bush," returns the new person to his family, and there is a joyful celebration involving dancing, feasting, and music. The boy puts on the tribal gown—in many cases, a long embroidered shirt. In the graduation festival for girls they become the chief performers in the dancing and singing, and at the end of the festival they are judged on how well they have learned the skills they were taught. Parents exchange gifts with their children. The event ends with the ritual of putting on a woman's *lappas*, headdress, and beads.

BIRTH RITUALS

There are songs and rituals associated with childbirth in rural Liberia. Tribes that have secret societies often have a special house for childbirth, where Sande women help in the delivery. Childbirth is still risky in Liberia, and a successful delivery is accompanied by dances and songs to protect the child and its mother. If the child is related to the village chief, the celebrations are very grand.

FUNERAL CELEBRATIONS

The funeral procession of a Bassa *zoe*.

Like other aspects of Liberian life, the complex rituals associated with burying the dead have altered with the war and the influence of Islam and Christianity. Modern funeral rituals often involve both African songs and Christian hymns or Islamic chants.

Traditional funeral ceremonies, especially among tribes in Sande and Poro societies, often lasted many days. The body was held for three or four days under the eaves of the palaver hut. On those days the men of the Dei tribe would dance the *ziawa* (zee-AH-wah), called *gbaa* (geh-BAH) in some languages, while the women stayed indoors. When a Sande *zoe* died, similar songs and dances were performed for three days. Although many of these ceremonies are now rare, some of the songs have been recorded.

The festival to honor the death of a chief is a big affair. It might take up to two years to prepare for, and when it does take place it includes a celebration for the new chief. The long period of preparation is to give the family time to save for the enormous cost of the event. A cow must be killed, neighboring chiefs are invited, and fine clothes and accomplished dancers must be found.

Decoration Day marks the day when people of various religions go to the graveyards to decorate and tidy their family's graves.

FOOD

LIBERIAN FOOD HAS SIMILARITIES with other West African cuisines, in which cassava root and rice are the staples of most meals. In Liberia, however, there is a long tradition of cooking brought to the country by Americo-Liberians as well as the influence of Western expatriates.

STAPLES

Both types of rice, wet and dry, can be grown in Liberia without the complex irrigation systems that are used in other countries. Rice and cassava are grown in every rural household and sold in the city markets.

Cassava is an edible root that has few nutrients but thrives in the damp climate of Liberia. It has the advantage that it can be left in the ground until it is needed. Other starchy foods grown in the country include *eddoes* (taro, an edible root), plantains, sweet corn, and sweet potatoes. The pulp of palm nuts is also an important staple in the Liberian diet.

MEAT

Meat is a luxury in the villages, and hunting and fishing are the main sources of supply. Game includes antelope, wild pigs, and even leopards, while other sources of protein are lizards, snakes, frogs, termites, and snails. Smaller animals are caught in traps. A common practice is for women and children to go down to the river, where the children get into the water and make a noise to frighten the fish downstream. The women wait for the fish with small nets and trap them as they move away from the noise. When men fish in the streams, they use a hook and line or they may poison a pool with sasswood

Above: **Fresh fruits and vegetables being sold at a village market.**

Opposite: **Two women balancing dishes of fresh fish on their heads in downtown Monrovia.**

ANANSE AND THE FRUIT OF THE FOREST

One day Ananse the spider decided to accompany a village girl as she looked for food in the forest. She was a good gatherer and knew all the best secret places to find good things to eat. First she went to where there was a small fruit tree with a few ripe fruits. Ananse pushed past her and ate them all up. The girl sighed and went to the next place she knew, a banana grove with small but sweet bananas. Ananse grabbed them all and ate them up again.

The girl got irritated with Ananse and decided to teach him a lesson. She took him deep into the bush, where she knew there was a colony of honey bees inside a tree stump. She showed Ananse the big combs of honey, and although he was really full with fruit he jumped inside the stump and started eating. Soon he was swollen with honey, and when he tried to get out of the tree stump he found he was stuck. "Help me," he cried, "I can't get out."

"Not likely," said the girl, who went off to a place where she knew there were some huge cassavas that she could dig up for her family. Ananse called for help, but he was deep in the forest where no one could hear him.

Dried antelope meat being sold at a market in Monrovia.

Bugabug, *or termites, are eaten either raw or roasted in Liberia.*

bark. This stuns the fish but does not make them poisonous to eat. Fish are eaten fresh or dried. Chickens are kept but are saved for their eggs and for sacrifices, and goat is a popular meat in the cities. Cattle are a luxury and are slaughtered only for important festivals.

OTHER FOODS

Liberia has many types of fresh produce. A wide variety of vegetables is grown in kitchen gardens, including cucumbers, okra, collard greens, lima beans, and cabbage. Onions, *eddoes*, chili peppers, coconuts, ginger, eggplants, tomatoes, and other vegetables thrive in the Liberian climate. Sweet potato leaves and cassava leaves are boiled and eaten as vegetables, while cassava is prepared in a traditional, labor-intensive way—by soaking and pounding it before cooking.

Fruit is also plentiful and includes soursop, grapefruit, mangoes, oranges, pineapples, bananas, and watermelons. Peanuts are used in baking cakes and cookies as well as in a savory sauce. Also cultivated in the kitchen garden are kola trees. The kola nut is of no value as a food, but it is chewed as a stimulant because it contains caffeine.

A TYPICAL LIBERIAN MEAL

Rice is normally eaten boiled, with a spicy sauce that may contain meat. Sometimes it is cooked into a kind of risotto called *jollof* (JOH-lof), with meat and vegetables. A seasonal alternative to rice is cassava, cooked into a porridge with other vegetables and meat or made into little boat-shaped cakes that are used to scoop up the accompanying stew. Other common dishes are *fufu* (FOO-foo), a fermented cassava porridge, and *dumboy* (DUM-boy), the unfermented version. These are served with palm butter and vegetables. *Tumborgee* (tum-BOR-gee), or fermented palm butter, is common in Lofah. Palm butter and *tumborgee* are served more as a stew than a sauce and often contain meat, beans, onions, or vegetables in season. Frog soup is quite common, and deep-fried vegetables, fish, and termites (called *bugabug*) are popular.

A LIBERIAN FEAST

In a Liberian feast all the dishes are set out together. Nothing is cleared away during the meal, and no new dishes are brought in. The centerpiece may be a roasted animal. *Dumboy* and *fufu* form the base of the meal. With them are palm butter, palaver sauce (a meat stew made with spinach leaves), or *tumborgee*. Goat soup and "check rice" (rice and okra) are also served. Meat dishes might be pig's trotter (the cooked foot of a pig) with cabbage, fish with sweet potato leaves, and shrimp with palm nuts. Fried plantains and organ soup, the national dishes, are

A woman portioning out a meal of rice and stew.

In Liberia, dishes are not usually served in courses, but instead all together, so the diners may combine their food and pick and choose the foods they want.

likely to be present. Vegetable dishes include Monrovian collards and cabbage cooked in a soup with bacon, chili, and onions. Dessert may be fruit, cakes, rice bread, or sweet potato pone. In a village feast, utensils consist of spoons, bowls, and plates. In a city feast, there are Western utensils with glasses and a place setting for each guest.

EATING OUT

All over Liberia there are small eating places known as cookshops. Country chop, their most famous dish, consists of meat, fish, and greens fried in palm oil. In the markets, street stalls sell deep-fried foods and cooked seafood. In Monrovia the dining establishments range from cookshops to gourmet restaurants serving French or Italian cuisine. Somewhere between the two are U.S.-influenced restaurants serving hamburgers, American breakfasts, and fried chicken alongside Liberian dishes such as *bong* fries (fried cassava chips).

Cookshops serve local food: basic Liberian staples with spicy sauces and stews.

A woman sells home-made drinks in recycled bottles.

There are also many small Lebanese restaurants selling hummus, *fuul* (FU-ul, a salad made of beans and olive oil), *khobez* (KOH-bez, Lebanese bread), and pastries such as baklava. Indian restaurants are also numerous in the cities. Another import from the West is the many pastry shops that sell cookies, cakes, chocolate, and ice cream. A popular local cake is Monrovian coconut pie, made with grated coconut meat, milk, and eggs. Many local ice creams are available, made with fresh fruit, eggs, and milk.

BEVERAGES

Popular drinks in Liberia include bottled beer made in Monrovia, palm wine made from fermented palm fruit, ginger beer, and a rum made from sugarcane. Milk is rarely drunk, and coffee drinking is only popular in the towns.

Palm wine is made by collecting the sap from palm trees. It is left in a calabash—a hollowed-out gourd hardened in the sun—where natural

Women carry firewood on their heads to the kitchen, in preparation for a communal feast.

yeasts collect on it. Fermentation is rapid. The drink is first very sweet and fizzy, then it turns alcoholic, and in two weeks it becomes a sour wine. It is a valuable village product, and some people keep many palm trees for this purpose. Palm wine is an essential part of celebrations and public village meetings. It can be used as currency, as part payment of a bride price, and as taxes paid to a chief. A kola nut is often sucked while palm wine is drunk, since kola acts as a stimulant and is said to keep the head clear.

KITCHEN EQUIPMENT

In the villages the basic means of cooking is an open fire outside the hut at the back of the building. The hearth is made of three flat stones, with the fire inside. A large iron cooking pot rests on the stones. Equipment for stirring the food is made locally from wood and is rarely bought or made of metal.

A large log of wood is fashioned into an hourglass shape and hollowed out to provide a container, which is used for pounding cassava with a thick wooden pole. Covers for food are woven from palm fiber or, in the bigger towns, made of plastic. Fishing nets, another vital piece of equipment, are also made from palm fiber. Plastic buckets and enamel bowls are often part of a dowry, and the iron cooking pot is an object of great value.

When water is collected a long distance from the village, a rod is held across the shoulders to balance two containers. The traditional container is a calabash, but sometimes buckets are used.

Every piece of kitchen equipment is treasured, and very few things are thrown away. Empty produce cans are reused as cooking pots, and glass jars are a rare luxury. If a woman divorces her husband she takes her cooking utensils with her, because they represent the true value of her wealth.

At mealtime most people eat with either their hands or a carved wooden spoon. At big feasts there are no dishes—each person helps him- or herself from the common dishes—but at home the food is distributed into bowls when the meal starts. The bowls are either homemade from wood or are made of the more precious plastic or enamel and bought from the market.

In the cities the degree of sophistication of the kitchen varies enormously—from fairly modern gas stoves and refrigerators in the houses of the very rich to charcoal fires outside the house, often in a small, open-roofed hut that is separate from the main building. A butane gas cylinder is a sign of a well-to-do family, as are drinking glasses, factory-made plates, and metal knives and forks.

Women pounding wheat to prepare *kala*, a deep-fried dish they may later sell at the market.

LIBERIAN SWEET POTATO PONE

3 cups (750 ml) grated raw sweet potatoes
1 cup (250 ml) molasses or dark syrup
2 teaspoons (10 ml) ground ginger
2 teaspoons (10 ml) baking powder
1 teaspoon (5 ml) salt
1/3 cup (85 ml) vegetable oil

Combine all the ingredients and simmer slowly, stirring constantly, for 10 minutes. Pour into a well-greased 9-inch (23-cm) baking pan. Bake at 325 degrees F (160 degrees C) for 30 minutes, stirring every 5 minutes for the first 20 minutes to ensure that the mixture is evenly combined. Smooth down the top and allow to brown. Cut into squares and serve either hot or cold.

STEWED MANGO WITH CLOVES

4 large mangoes
1 cup (250 ml) corn syrup
6 whole cloves

Peel and cut the mangoes and place the slices in a large saucepan. Add corn syrup and cloves and simmer the mixture for 15 minutes or until mangoes are tender. Cool and serve. This simple fruit dessert can be eaten after dinner or as an evening snack.

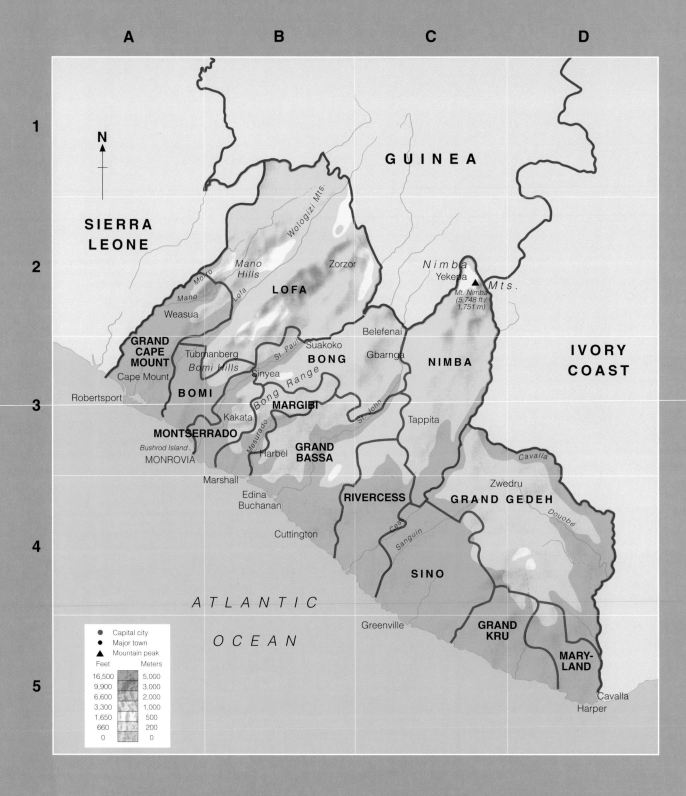

MAP OF LIBERIA

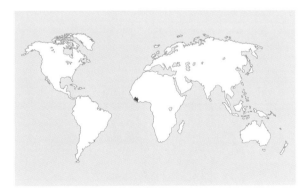

ECONOMIC LIBERIA

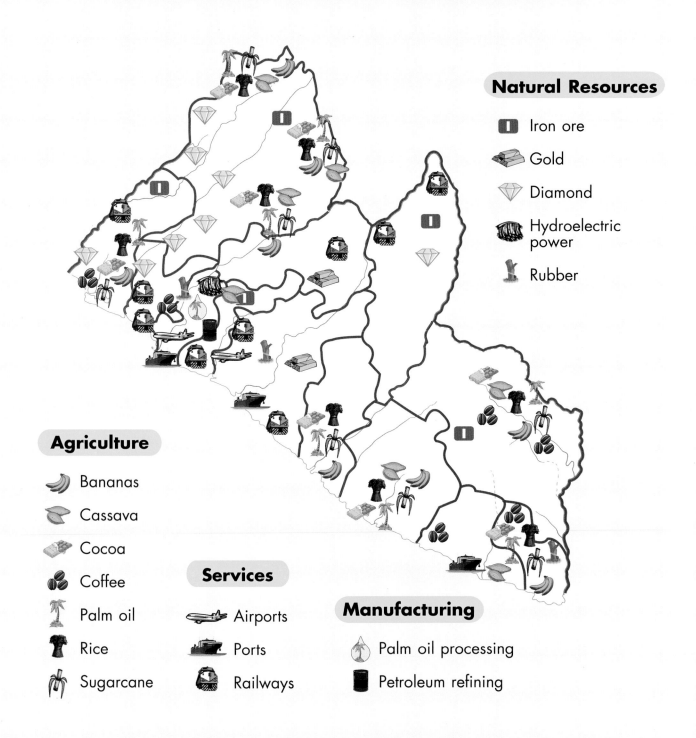

Natural Resources

- Iron ore
- Gold
- Diamond
- Hydroelectric power
- Rubber

Agriculture

- Bananas
- Cassava
- Cocoa
- Coffee
- Palm oil
- Rice
- Sugarcane

Services

- Airports
- Ports
- Railways

Manufacturing

- Palm oil processing
- Petroleum refining

ABOUT
THE ECONOMY

OVERVIEW

Civil war and mismanagement of the country under the regime of Charles Taylor have left the economy and infrastructure of Liberia in a poor state. Many businesses have fled the country, and the new government under President Johnson-Sirleaf has a huge challenge in rebuilding the economy and attracting foreign businesses to invest. However, Liberia is rich in natural resources, especially minerals and forestry, and it has a climate that is ideal for certain kinds of agriculture, such as rubber trees. To rebuild the country's economy, Liberia will need much assistance from foreign companies and experts in redeveloping rubber, timber, and diamond mining—the most profitable sectors of the economy.

GROSS DOMESTIC PRODUCT (GDP)

$902.9 million (U.S.)

GDP PER CAPITA

$500 (U.S.)

GROWTH RATE

8.5 percent

GDP BY SECTOR

Agriculture: 76.9 percent
Industry: 5.4 percent
Services: 17.7 percent

CURRENCY

1 U.S. dollar = 59.43 Liberian dollars (2006 estimate)

UNEMPLOYMENT RATE

85 percent (2003 estimate)

MAIN PRODUCTS

Bananas, cassava, cocoa, coffee, rice, palm oil, sugarcane, sheep, goats, diamonds, gold, iron ore, corn, rubber, timber

LABOR FORCE BY OCCUPATION

Agriculture: 70 percent
Industry and manufacturing: 8 percent
Services: 22 percent

MAIN EXPORTS

Rubber, timber, iron ore, diamonds, cocoa, coffee

MAIN TRADE PARTNERS

Exports: Germany (40.1 percent), South Africa (12 percent), Poland (11.7 percent), United States (8.5 percent), Spain (8.2 percent) (2006 estimate) Imports: South Korea (43.2 percent), Singapore (15 percent), Japan (12.8 percent), China (8.2 percent)

TELECOMMUNICATIONS

Telephone lines in use: 6,900 (2002 estimate)
Mobile phones: 160,000 (2005 estimate)
Internet users: 1,000 (2002 estimate)

AIRPORTS

53 (two with paved runways) (2007)

RAILWAYS

304 miles (490 km)

MERCHANT MARINE

1,948 ships of more than 1,000 gross registered tons

CULTURAL LIBERIA

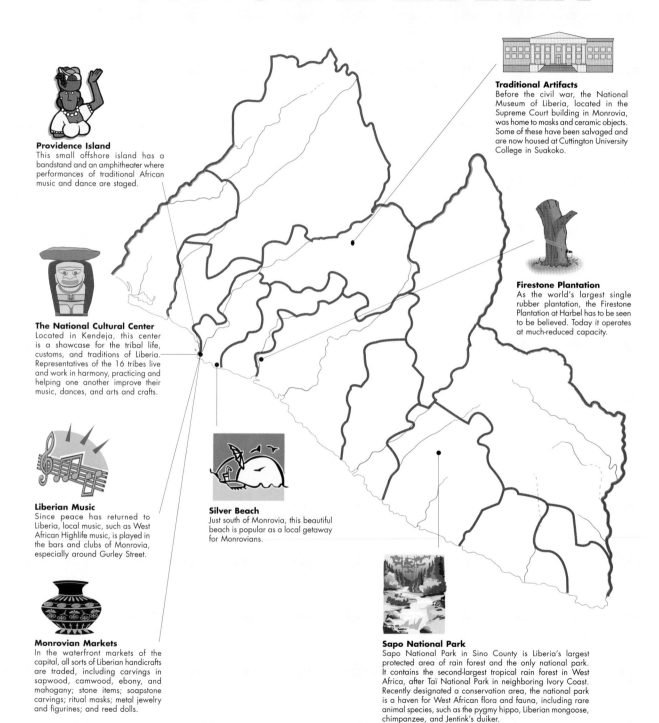

Providence Island
This small offshore island has a bandstand and an amphitheater where performances of traditional African music and dance are staged.

The National Cultural Center
Located in Kendeja, this center is a showcase for the tribal life, customs, and traditions of Liberia. Representatives of the 16 tribes live and work in harmony, practicing and helping one another improve their music, dances, and arts and crafts.

Liberian Music
Since peace has returned to Liberia, local music, such as West African Highlife music, is played in the bars and clubs of Monrovia, especially around Gurley Street.

Monrovian Markets
In the waterfront markets of the capital, all sorts of Liberian handicrafts are traded, including carvings in sapwood, camwood, ebony, and mahogany; stone items; soapstone carvings; ritual masks; metal jewelry and figurines; and reed dolls.

Silver Beach
Just south of Monrovia, this beautiful beach is popular as a local getaway for Monrovians.

Traditional Artifacts
Before the civil war, the National Museum of Liberia, located in the Supreme Court building in Monrovia, was home to masks and ceramic objects. Some of these have been salvaged and are now housed at Cuttington University College in Suakoko.

Firestone Plantation
As the world's largest single rubber plantation, the Firestone Plantation at Harbel has to be seen to be believed. Today it operates at much-reduced capacity.

Sapo National Park
Sapo National Park in Sino County is Liberia's largest protected area of rain forest and the only national park. It contains the second-largest tropical rain forest in West Africa, after Taï National Park in neighboring Ivory Coast. Recently designated a conservation area, the national park is a haven for West African flora and fauna, including rare animal species, such as the pygmy hippo, Liberian mongoose, chimpanzee, and Jentink's duiker.

ABOUT THE CULTURE

OFFICIAL NAME
Republic of Liberia

NATIONALITY
Liberian

FLAG DESCRIPTION
Eleven equal horizontal stripes of red alternating with white, with a white five-pointed star on a blue square in the upper left corner. The design is based closely on the U.S. flag.

CAPITAL
Monrovia

LAND AREA
37,189 square miles (96,320 sq km)

MAJOR TOWNS
Buchanan, Edina, Greenville, Harper, Marshall, Robertsport, Yekepa

POPULATION
3,195,931 (2007)

BIRTHRATE
43.75 per thousand population

DEATH RATE
22.24 per thousand population

POPULATION GROWTH RATE
4.836 percent (2007)

LIFE EXPECTANCY
Total population: 40.39 years
Male: 38.93 years
Female: 41.89 years (2007 estimate)

INFANT MORTALITY RATE
Total: 149.73 deaths/1,000 live births
Male: 165.65 deaths/1,000 live births
Female: 133.34 deaths/1,000 live births (2007 estimate)

ADMINISTRATIVE DISTRICTS (COUNTIES)
Bomi, Bong, Gbarpolu, Grand Bassa, Grand Cape Mount, Grand Gedeh, Grand Kru, Lofah, Margibi, Maryland, Montserrado, Nimba, River Cess, River Gee, Sinoe

HIGHEST POINT
Mount Nimba at Guest House Hill
(5,748 ft/1,752 m)

HEAD OF STATE
President Ellen Johnson-Sirleaf

MAJOR RIVERS
Saint Paul, Lofa

LANGUAGES
English, plus 30 or more indigenous languages

RELIGIONS
Christianity (40%), Islam (20%), animism (40%)

TRIBES
Bassa, Bella, Dei, Gbandi, Gio, Gola, Grebo, Kissi, Kpelle, Krahn, Kru, Loma, Mandingo, Mano, Mende, Vai

TIME LINE

IN LIBERIA	IN THE WORLD

IN LIBERIA

1460s
Portuguese traders arrive along the Grain Coast (now Liberia).

1822
The American Colonization Society begins the process of helping freed slaves return to Africa. The first group of colonists lands at Cape Mesurado and founds Monrovia.

1824
The colonists adopt the name of Liberia for their new country.

1847
A constitution modeled on that of the United States is drawn up. Liberia is the first African colony to become an independent state. By this time more than 10,000 free blacks have moved there. Joseph Jenkins Roberts is elected the first president of the new state.

1943
William Tubman is elected president of Liberia.

1951
Women and property owners vote in the presidential election for the first time.

1971
William Tubman dies and is succeeded by William Tolbert Jr.

1980
Master Sergeant Samuel Doe stages a military coup and Tolbert is assassinated. A People's Redemption Council headed by Doe suspends the constitution and takes power.

1985
Doe wins election amid accusations of vote-rigging.

1989
The National Patriotic Front of Liberia (NPFL) led by Charles Taylor begins an uprising against the government.

1990
Amid an escalating civil war, the Economic Community of West African States (ECOWAS) sends peacekeeping forces.
Doe is executed by members of the NPFL.

IN THE WORLD

1776
U.S. Declaration of Independence

1789–99
The French Revolution

1869
The Suez Canal is opened.

1914
World War I begins.

1939
World War II begins.

1949
The North Atlantic Treaty Organization (NATO) is formed.

1966–69
The Chinese Cultural Revolution

1986
Nuclear power disaster at Chernobyl in Ukraine

IN LIBERIA	IN THE WORLD
1991 ECOWAS and the NPFL agree to disarm and set up an Interim Government of National Unity.	**1991** Breakup of the Soviet Union
1994 The warring factions agree to a timetable for disarmament and the setting up of a joint Council of State.	
1996 Fighting resumes and spreads to Monrovia.	
1997 Charles Taylor wins a landslide victory in presidential elections and his National Patriotic Party wins a majority in the National Assembly.	**1997** Hong Kong is returned to China.
1999 Ghana and Nigeria accuse Liberia of supporting Revolutionary United Front rebels in Sierra Leone. Rebel forces thought to have come from Guinea attack the town of Voinjama. Fighting displaces more than 25,000 Liberians.	
2000 Liberian forces launch a "massive offensive" against rebels in the north.	**2001** Terrorists crash planes in New York, Washington, D.C., and Pennsylvania.
2002 Taylor declares a state of emergency.	
2003 Rebels advance to within 6 miles (10 km) of Monrovia. President Taylor is accused of war crimes and is forced to leave the country. The interim government and rebels sign a peace accord in Ghana. Gyude Bryant is chosen to head the interim administration.	**2003** War in Iraq begins.
2005 Ellen Johnson-Sirleaf becomes the first woman to be elected as an African head of state. She takes office in January 2006.	
2006 Former president Charles Taylor appears before a UN-backed court in Sierra Leone on charges of crimes against humanity.	
2007 Charles Taylor's war crimes trial begins in The Hague.	

GLOSSARY

Aladura
An African Christian church.

Americo-Liberian
Liberians of African-American descent. These people can trace their ancestry to the freed slaves who settled in Liberia in the 19th century.

Ananse
Spider that figures in African stories.

calabash
Container made from a hollowed gourd.

Congo
People descended from freed slaves.

Creole
Language that amalgamates two others.

dumboy (DUM-boy)
Unfermented cassava porridge.

fufu (FOO-foo)
Fermented cassava porridge.

Go Ge
Arbiter of village disputes.

Krio
Creole language spoken in Sierra Leone.

kwi (KWEE)
Pidgin English for "foreigner."

Malinke
Language spoken by the Mandingo.

mancala (man-KAH-lah)
Board game played with counters.

mar kee ke nuu (mar KEY kay new)
Questioners prepared by a storyteller in between episodes of the story.

nenya (NEN-yah)
Gola children's game.

palaver hut
Place where village councils meet.

pelee (PEL-ee)
Music, dance, and performance festival.

Poro
Male secret society.

Sande
Female secret society.

syllabary
A kind of alphabet consisting of a character for each combination of vowel and consonant, or syllable.

to nuu (toh NEW)
Rich and powerful African leader; translates into English as "big shot."

tumborgee (tum-BOR-gee)
Fermented palm butter.

zoe (ZOH)
Priest, usually the head of Poro or Sande society.

FURTHER INFORMATION

BOOKS

Baughan, Brian. *Liberia (Africa: Continent in the Balance)*. Broomall, PA: Mason Crest Publishers, 2008.

Gay, John. *Red Dust on the Green Leaves: A Kpelle Twins' Childhood*. Thompson, CT: InterCulture Associates, 1973. (New paperback ed. in 2002 by New World African Press, Northridge, CA)

Miller, Debra A. *Liberia*. San Diego: Lucent Books, 2004.

Olukoju, Ayodeji Oladimeji. *Culture and Customs of Liberia (Culture and Customs of Africa)*. Westport, CT: Greenwood Press, 2006.

Streissguth, Thomas. *Liberia in Pictures (Visual Geography)*. Minneapolis: Lerner Publishing Group, 2006.

WEBSITES

www.allafrica.com/liberia/
www.animalinfo.org/country/liberia.htm
www.bong-town.com/
www.cia.gov/library/publications/the-world-factbook/geos/li.html
www.liberiaenvironmentalwatch.org/Home.asp
www.iucn.org
www.liberianforum.com
www.liberianobserver.com
www.liberianonline.com/
www.nationsencyclopedia.com/Africa/Liberia-ENVIRONMENT.html
www.news.bbc.co.uk1/hi/world/africa/country_profiles/1043500.stm
www.unicef.org/infobycountry/liberia/
www.wildinvest.com/hippo.html

FILMS

Daniel Junge (Dir.). *Iron Ladies of Liberia*, 2007.

Jonathan Stack and James Brabazon (Dir.). *Liberia: An Uncivil War*, 2004.

MUSIC

Arthur Alberts. *Songs of the African Coast: Cafe Music of Liberia*. Yarngo, LLC, 2007.

Classic Highlife. Aim, 2004.

George Weah and Epee and Koum. *Lone Star Liberia*. Sonodisc, 1999.

Liberia: The Music of Vai Islam. Multicultural Media, 2007.

BIBLIOGRAPHY

Boe, P. Nathaniel. *Miracle on the Atlantic Coast: How to Transform Liberia into a Peaceful and Prosperous Country*. Bloomington, IN: AuthorHouse, 2007.

Boone, Clinton C. *Liberia as I Know It*. Southfield, MI: Written Images, 2006.

Greene, Graham. *Journey Without Maps*. London: Penguin Classics, 2006.

Horace, Selena Gennehma. *African Recipes: The Liberian Cuisine*. Washington, DC: Horasel Productions, 2003.

McPherson, J.H.T. *History of Liberia*. Kila, MT: Kessinger Publishing Co., 2004.

Meadows, David E. *Liberia*. New York: Berkley Books, 2003.

Moran, Mary H. *Liberia: The Violence of Democracy*. Philadelphia: University of Pennsylvania Press, 2006.

Sankawulo, Wilton. *Sundown at Dawn: A Liberian Odyssey*. Houston: Dusty Spark Publishing, 2005.

Watkins, Samuel R. *Liberia Communication*. Bloomington, IN: AuthorHouse, 2007.

INDEX